The Transfer of Criminal Proceedings in the European Union

The Transfer of Criminal Proceedings in the European Union

An exploration of the current practice and of possible ways for improvement, based on practitioners' views

Pieter Verrest
Michael Lindemann
Paul Mevis
Sanne Salverda

eleven

This project was funded by the European Union's Justice Programme (2014-2020), JUST-AG-2019, under grant agreement 88185

Project acronym: TROP

Published, sold and distributed by Eleven
P.O. Box 85576
2508 CG The Hague
The Netherlands
Tel.: +31 70 33 070 33
Fax: +31 70 33 070 30
e-mail: sales@elevenpub.nl
www.elevenpub.com

Sold and distributed in USA and Canada
Independent Publishers Group
814 N. Franklin Street
Chicago, IL 60610, USA
Order Placement: +1 800 888 4741
Fax: +1 312 337 5985
orders@ipgbook.com
www.ipgbook.com

Eleven is an imprint of Boom uitgevers Den Haag.

ISBN 978-94-6236-314-4
ISBN 978-94-0011-163-9 (E-book)

Table of Contents

Foreword

This report marks the final stage of the TROP research project. It presents the results of our research, conducted over the past two years, into the practice of the transfer of criminal proceedings in the judicial cooperation in the EU. The project was funded by the European Commission under the Justice Programme.

It has been an experience that we have enjoyed in every respect: from working in a multidisciplinary research team, to having in-depth discussions with experts during our on-site visits and discussing proposals for improvement during the Working Conferences. We met many inspiring European professionals, with passion for their work.

We would like to express our gratitude to all respondents from the participating Member States, as well as to all were vitally important. In fact, they confirmed our research philosophy: ideas for improving judicial cooperation and the preparation of possible new instruments should be based on a bottom-up approach. They can be developed on the experiences and ideas of practitioners, and then elaborated and cross checked in a discussion between experts, policy makers and scholars.

Although not every member of the research team took part in writing this final report, in every aspect it represents the result of our work together as a team. This includes Hannah Lucas, who assisted in the organisation of the Working Conferences.

We have chosen to present the results of our research in a concise and easy-to-read report. Obviously, we hope that the report may contribute to fruitful discussions and negotiations on a future new legal instrument on the transfer of criminal proceedings in the EU.

Rotterdam/Amsterdam/Bielefeld, 30 May 2022

The TROP research team,

Pieter Verrest
Paul Mevis
Sanne Salverda
Vivianne Mooren
Kasper van der Schaft
Nynke Bakkenes
Leonie Lunshof
Ylonka Zwaan
Michael Lindemann

Group picture

Figure 1 **The participants in the Second Working Conference of the TROP project; Rotterdam 7 April 2022**

1 Introduction

1.1 The transfer of criminal proceedings between Member States

The judicial cooperation in criminal matters in the European Union has seen considerable progress over the last two decades. This is at least in part due to the development of a comprehensive dedicated legal framework. This framework has been created based on the principle of mutual recognition of judicial decisions and has brought such instruments as the European Arrest Warrant (EAW) and the European Investigation Order (EIO).

The legal framework provides the judicial authorities with easy-to-use solutions for their daily work in taking on – in close cooperation with their colleague judicial authorities in other Member States – cross border elements in criminal cases. There is however one notable exception to this: in the EU legal framework an instrument for the transfer of criminal proceedings is lacking.

The transfer of criminal proceedings is a form of judicial cooperation wherein the judicial authority of a Member State is of the opinion that a criminal case could best be prosecuted in another Member State. To that end, the judicial authority sends a request for the transfer of criminal proceedings to the competent authority of the other recipient Member State.

There is some ambiguity surrounding the transfer of criminal proceedings. One hears judicial authorities complaining about the lack of clarity that is caused by the absence of a specific instrument. In most cases, they must rely on a very general legal basis for requesting the transfer of criminal proceedings – Article 21 of the 1959 Council of Europe Convention on mutual legal assistance. A dedicated Council of Europe Convention, the Convention on the Transfer of Proceedings in Criminal Matter (1972), has been ratified by less than half of the EU Member States. Even between Member States that are parties to the 1972 Convention, it is not always used. That leaves judicial authorities without proper guidance about the procedure to follow. It also leaves them in uncertainty whether their request will be followed up, let alone if and when they will get an answer to their request. This discourages authorities to consider transferring proceedings.

On the other hand, as a requested authority, in fact the same judicial authorities, tend to prefer a large degree of discretion concerning the decision to accept a request for the transfer of proceedings and take over a criminal case from the authorities of the requesting Member State. This enables them to take aboard all kinds of considerations in their decision, including those related to a proper allocation of their scarce capacity.

There has been an attempt to create an EU legal instrument for the transfer of criminal proceedings. In 2009, a Member States initiative from Sweden and 14 other Member States for a Council Framework Decision on the transfer of proceedings in criminal matters was introduced.[1] It was tabled for discussion in a Council Working group, which failed to reach an agreement on the content. This was partly due to the fact that just before the Lisbon Treaty came into force, time for negotiations was limited. It should also be remembered that under the Third Pillar of the Amsterdam Treaty, unanimity was required. Nevertheless, the failure was also due to the existence of profound disagreement between Member States delegations on pivotal elements like jurisdiction.

1.2 The research project

The idea for a research project into the transfer of criminal proceedings came up in a discussion between the Amsterdam Public Prosecution office and Erasmus School of Law at the beginning of 2019. At that time, the then Romanian presidency of the EU drew attention to the absence of an instrument for the transfer of criminal proceedings, referring to the 2009 Swedish initiative for a Council Framework Decision.[2]

In our analysis, the transfer of proceedings can be a very useful tool in the practice of judicial cooperation between Member States. But also, a tool that we and others[3] felt needed improvement. It can be a useful alternative to solutions such as the issuing of an EAW, which are more complex to process and are very intrusive for the persons involved. The transfer of proceedings may in other situations help prevent impunity when, for example, the perpetrators of a minor offence have returned to their home state after committing the offence – an EAW is not possible for minor offences.

1 2009/C 219/03.
2 Doc. 9728/19.
3 See f.e. Eurojust, *Report on Eurojust's casework in the field of prevention and resolution of conflicts of jurisdiction*, 2018, p. 11-13 and B. de Jonge, Transfer of criminal proceedings: from stumbling block to cornerstone of cooperation in criminal matters in the EU, *ERA Forum* 21 (2020), p. 449-464.

As experts in the field of judicial cooperation, the team members of the Amsterdam Public Prosecution office wanted to improve the effectiveness of the transfer of proceedings. The prospect of a research project into the transfer of criminal proceedings received wide support from EJN colleagues in other Member States.

Together with Bielefeld University and the Belgian Federal Prosecution Office, Erasmus School of Law and the Amsterdam Public Prosecution office decided to apply for EU funding for a research project into the current practice of transferring proceedings between Member States and possible ways for improvement (TROP). Funding for the project was granted in October 2019 as part of the European Union's Justice Programme (2014-2020).[4]

During our project, we learned that the European Commission was planning to propose a new EU legislative instrument on the Transfer of criminal proceedings in Q3 of 2022.[5] This followed up discussions in the Council in December 2020.[6] It was also decided that the results of the TROP research project should be awaited.[7]

This makes our research project and its results even more relevant. Of course, our research project was conducted independently from the preparatory works of the European Commission. But on occasion, we were happy to share some preliminary results with experts from the European Commission.

1.3 The subject matter

The aim of our research project is to develop proposals for the improvement of the transfer of proceedings in criminal matters in the EU, based on the experience and views of practitioners in the field of judicial cooperation.

The central question in the research project is:

What is the current practice of the transfer of criminal proceedings in the European Union and how could it be improved?

In order to explore the central question, we have formulated three sub-questions, that will be answered consecutively:
- What is the current practice of the transfer of criminal proceedings in the participating Member States?

4 JUST-AG-2019, grant agreement no. 88185.
5 Commission Work programme 2022, COM (2021) 645 final, annex I, p. 3.
6 See Council conclusions 'The European arrest warrant and extradition procedures – current challenges and the way forward', 2020/C 419/09.
7 Ibid. par. 38.

- What are the main challenges experienced in the practice of the transfer of criminal proceedings?
- What could be solutions for the identified challenges, with an aim to improve the transfer of criminal proceedings?

At the start of the research project, we wanted to keep open different options with regard to the form in which the improvement should be achieved. Improvement could be embodied by establishing best practices as well as by a new legislative instrument. As already mentioned, during the research project it became clear that the European Commission would elaborate a proposal for a new legal instrument; the focus of the research project was adjusted accordingly. In the research for the third sub-question, we especially focused on possible solutions in the framework of a legal instrument.

1.4 Research design

Research partners

In the research project, Erasmus School of Law acted as the project leader. Erasmus School of Law's expertise includes comparative criminal law, policy and law making in an EU perspective. The Amsterdam Public Prosecution Office provided its extensive experience in judicial cooperation in the European Union, including the transfer of criminal proceedings. It also contributed with prior experience in conducting research on the verge of practice and the legal framework[8] and its close network of judicial experts in the Member States.

Bielefeld University delivered additional scientific input, notably in the areas of comparative criminal law, fundamental rights and empirical research.

The Belgian Federal Public Prosecution Office took part in several brainstorming sessions that shaped the project and determined its content. Unfortunately, the Federal Public Prosecution Office had to withdraw from participating in the interviews and in the organisation of the Working Conferences due to a lack of staff resources.

Together, we acted as a multidisciplinary research team. Experience with the transfer of criminal proceedings in the practice of judicial cooperation, experience in the field of law making and policy making, and scientific expertise went hand in hand. This allowed for a comprehensive analysis of the research material at every stage of the project.

---

8 See J.J. Arends e.al., *A comparative analysis of the implementation of Article 4(6) Framework Decision 2002/548: Resocialization above surrender?*, Amsterdam 2017 (JUST/2014/JCOO/AG/CRIM/7739).

Participating Member States

Throughout the project, we could rely on the dedicated collaboration of a network of expert respondents from nine Member States participating in this research project: Austria, Belgium,[9] France, Germany, the Netherlands, Poland, Romania, Spain and Sweden. Experts included members of (general) public prosecution offices, judges and public officials of ministries of Justice, with a background in judicial cooperation, policy making and law making.

Research philosophy

The research methodology that we used in this research project was specially developed for conducting research aimed at providing elements for the improvement of the EU legislative framework for judicial cooperation between Member States.

It departs from the idea that EU lawmakers sometimes lack real insight into practice and experience with daily challenges in the judicial cooperation between Member States. This may lead to poorly functioning legislation. This can be avoided if a bottom-up approach for law making is adopted. Experts from the different Member States tend to speak the same language rather than Member States representatives in a Working Group in the EU law-making process. Our philosophy is therefore that the discussion about improvement and possible new legislation should be initiated between experts from a substantial number of Member States.[10] This in-depth discussion can be prepared and guided by a research team that combines practical experience and theoretical knowledge. By integrating the perspectives of different professions from different Member States, the project uses the social science method of triangulation: the reconciliation of these different perspectives allows for a more detailed and differentiated picture of legal reality to emerge. Ideas for improvement may be abstracted from it. Subsequently, these ideas will be elaborated by the research team. Finally, the ideas will put into the form of proposals that will be cross checked and adapted in an open discussion between experts, scholars and policy makers/legislative lawyers. A concept of the report and its draft conclusions are then shared and discussed with the European Commission.

Research activity

We started in 2020 with the first part of the research (WP1), consisting of collecting and analysing literature, policy documents, legislation and other relevant material.

9 In the case of both Belgium and the Netherlands, we had expert respondents who were not members of the research team.

10 Explained in P. Verrest, *Europese Idealen*, The Hague: Boom juridisch 2016.

By that time, COVID 19 had disrupted work and had a considerable impact on working life – both in the professional area of the participating public prosecution officials and at the university, and for the research team and their respondents in the participating Member States. This caused some delay in the project. We managed to get back on schedule in the second half of 2020 and concluded WP1 by sending out a questionnaire to respondents in the nine participating Member States and receiving their input in response.

Based on the results in WP1, we started WP2 with an intermediary analysis. In several brainstorming meetings, the project team presented an initial image of the state of play of the transfer of criminal proceedings in the EU and of topics of interest. This resulted quite naturally in a comprehensive topic list for the semi-structured interviews we planned to conduct in the framework of on-site visits to the participating Member States. However, COVID 19 travel restrictions made it impossible to travel in the second quarter of 2021. We considered switching to online interviews via Zoom, but in the end were reluctant to do so. On-site visits and face-to-face contact enable in-depth discussion far more than the online environment. After waiting several months, it was finally possible to travel again. Between September and November 2021, we were able to visit the participating Member States and conduct the interviews. Each of the interviews involved four to six respondents from, as explained, different professional backgrounds. We conducted the interviews in different compositions of members of the research team. This was compensated by organising team briefings about the outcome of the interviews. The richness of the discussions during the on-site interviews made the waiting worthwhile.

During our project, several ideas for broadening the scope of the research emerged. An additional (online) interview was conducted with experts from Eurojust to incorporate their specialist views and experience. Eurojust has taken initiatives to promote a better use of the transfer of criminal proceedings.[11] We also conducted an online interview with a representative from the Bureau for Euregional cooperation (BES) to focus on the intensive daily practice of judicial cooperation between Belgium, Germany and the Netherlands and its particularities, in the Euregion Meuse-Rhine. Finally, two interviews with specialised defence lawyers provided some insight into considerations and wishes for improving the transfer of criminal proceedings from the perspective of the defence.

The COVID 19 restrictions in place at the end of 2021 and the beginning of 2022 made it impossible to organise a physical Working Conference. The Working Conference, central part of WP3, and open to experts and policy makers from all Member States and European Union institutions (not only the participating Member States) was

11 See for example Eurojust, *Report on Strategic seminar Conflicts of Jurisdiction, Transfer of Proceedings and Ne Bis In Idem: Successes, shortcomings and Solutions*, The Hague, 4 June 2015.

aimed at broadening the scope of the research project. It would serve as a validation of the challenges identified in the interviews in WP2 and provide the opportunity to discuss and cross check proposals for improvement in an interdisciplinary debate between experts, scholars and policy makers.

We found a solution by dividing the envisaged Working Conference into two parts: a first part dedicated to a discussion on the challenges identified in the on-site interviews (in an online Working Conference on 20 January 2022) and a second part aimed at discussing draft proposals for solutions with both experts from the field and policy makers and legislative lawyers (a physical Working Conference in Rotterdam on 7 April 2022). This turned out to be a successful approach.

The online Working Conference was attended by 34 experts from 21 Member States, as well as experts from Eurojust and the European Commission. It was animated with four different workshops in two rounds, to enable the participants to express their opinion about challenges in the field of improvement of the transfer of criminal proceedings.

The second, physical Working Conference took place in Rotterdam with – besides the members of the research team – a total of 40 participants from 23 Member States, Eurojust, the European Judicial Network, the European Commission, the General secretariat of the Council and academia. This conference was dedicated to discussing solutions for the challenges identified in the research project. In a plenary discussion, fundamental issues were addressed such as the mutual recognition character of a future legal instrument, jurisdiction and how to incorporate procedural rights. Subsequently, in four rounds of workshops, participants were given the opportunity to discuss and give their opinion on proposals for improving the transfer of criminal proceedings, drafted by the research team.

Figure 2 Flowchart Work Packages TROP research project

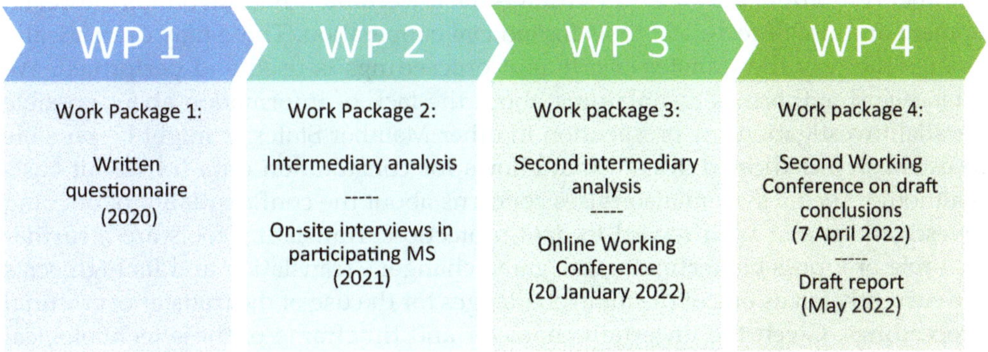

Limits of the research project

The research project had some limitations that we want to address here.

Firstly, as we knew beforehand, there is little literature about the transfer of proceedings in criminal matters. In addition, only a few policy documents regarding the current state of the transfer of proceedings in (Member States of) the EU exist. Besides an extensive study of the available literature and documents, we compensated the lack of written source information with comprehensive empirical research (including via the questionnaire, on-site visits and in-depth interviews). The same applies to statistical information about the number of incoming and outgoing requests for the transfer of criminal proceedings: that information proved to be very scarce. More detailed information about those requests (for example concerning the legal basis used and the authorities involved) and the way they were handled (think of time delays) was nearly absent. This means that most Member States do not have a complete picture of their own practice of transfer of criminal proceedings in this regard. Nevertheless, we were able to collect some statistics and to analyse them in general (see paragraph 3.2).

Furthermore, the influence of national law – implementing the international instruments adhered to by respective Member States – was sometimes difficult to grasp. We had to limit our research to the main characteristics of national law as provided to us and addressed in the interviews. It would have been interesting to further explore the effects of different legal cultures on the use of the transfer of criminal proceedings as a modality of judicial cooperation. Moreover, we would have been interested in further investigating, in a comparative perspective, the attainments of regional multilateral agreements that Member States have in place, such as the agreements between the Nordic states and between the Baltic states. However, that would have gone beyond the scope and the resources for the project.

Another restriction that we experienced is the uncertainty that surrounds the development and use of technical tools for judicial cooperation. These may dramatically change the way the transfer of criminal proceedings is used and performed. We often heard authorities complaining about the lack of information about possible parallel investigations or prosecution in other Member States. It might be possible to establish a dedicated system that allows for consultation on a hit/no hit basis – although such a system also raises concerns about the confidentiality of ongoing investigations and with regard to data protection. Translating tools are a further example of a possible technological 'game changer'. Translation and its high costs are currently felt as one of the main challenges for the use of the transfer of criminal proceedings. Given the uncertain character and timeframe of these technological innovations, we cannot incorporate them in our proposals for solutions for a good working instrument for the transfer of proceedings in criminal matters.

Finally, the project suffered some delays caused by the COVID 19 situation and the restrictions to travel and meetings. However, by the end of the research, we were confident that we had found alternative ways to uphold the quality of our research and to fully enjoy the results of our research methodology.

1.5 Content of this report

In chapter 2, we start the report with some general observations about the judicial cooperation in the European Union, that sketch in part the context of the transfer of criminal proceedings. Chapter 3 contains a description of the current practice of the transfer of criminal proceedings in the EU, based on empirical research. It looks at the legal instruments used to transfer proceedings as well as the different types of cases and situations where a transfer is considered by judicial authorities in the Member States. It also addresses the relation with the topic of conflicts of jurisdiction. Finally, it explains the influence that the adherence to a criminal justice system based on the legality principle, or the opportunity principle may have on the way judicial authorities perceive and use the transfer of criminal proceedings.

In chapter 4, some impressions are given of the challenges experienced while practising the transfer. Chapter 5 then contains proposals for solutions to those challenges. Different options are set out and explained, including their practical and policy making consequences.

1.6 Reading guidance

This report contains a short explanation of our research project and a presentation of its final results. It should be treated and read as a synthesis of the project.

As the reader will notice, the report does not contain citations of interviews or citations given by participants in the Working Conferences. We felt that it was necessary to promise this degree of confidentiality to our respondents, in exchange for their willingness to share their inside thoughts and views on the substance of our research topic and their personal experiences.

The aim of the report is to provide elements for the discussion on a future instrument in the law-making process of the EU. It is not our task or our ambition to present a comprehensive proposal for legislation. However, we hope that some of our proposals for improving the transfer of criminal proceedings may prove to be building stones for good functioning, dedicated EU legislation.

2 Some general observations about the judicial cooperation in the EU and the research project

2.1 Introduction

In the next chapters of this report, we will explain in detail our findings with regard to the transfer of criminal proceedings. But the wider context of the judicial cooperation between Member States is of equal importance when we aspire to improve the framework for the use of the transfer of proceedings. For that reason, we will share some general observations on the current status of the judicial cooperation in the EU. We start by presenting some preliminary reflections about the added value of the TROP project for the practice of judicial cooperation that we observed while conducting different research activities.

2.2 Effects of the research project

Throughout the project, we were struck by the enthusiasm in our project expressed by the experts from the participating Member States. This related to the topic of the research project, but also the research method. Authorities welcomed the opportunity that the project offered them to be involved and to contribute to ideas for improving the judicial cooperation in the EU in an open, *bottom-up* exercise. The on-site interviews led to the in-depth discussions that we had hoped for. We witnessed how authorities took the time to prepare themselves for the on-site interviews and their participation in the two Working Conferences, amongst other things by conducting internal surveys in their own Member State and sending out questionnaires.

One could say that the research project helped officials from the Member States to start their preparation for the future discussion on the European Commission's proposal for an instrument on the transfer of criminal proceedings.

Finally, we can point to some collateral benefits. The meetings between the research team and the respondents in the project made it possible to address other topics and clarify some issues in the daily practice of judicial cooperation between the Member States concerned. Those topics included the effect of case law of the Court of Justice on the judicial cooperation, and the start of the activity of the European Public Prosecution Office (EPPO). One topic that deserves particular attention is the appearance of the use of videoconferencing for trial purposes: videoconferencing is used as a means to have a suspect residing in Member State B stand trial before a court in Member State A. We have witnessed how this practice has rapidly developed and caused some disagreement between judicial cooperation experts and other judicial professionals.[12] It also raises questions about the relation between this modality and a future instrument on the transfer of criminal proceedings; see further in chapter 6.

2.3 Impressions of the daily practice of judicial cooperation

At several moments, respondents asked our attention for the lack of basic knowledge of judicial cooperation, including relevant EU legislation, among judicial authorities. As a matter of principle, every judicial authority in the Member States is supposed to possess a basic knowledge of EU legislation and to apply EU law on a case level. This does not alter the fact that judicial cooperation is generally considered to be a complicated topic and very much an experts' affair. Of course, judicial authorities confronted with a judicial cooperation issue can call on their expert colleagues within the public prosecution service or the judiciary for help. But this is not always practical or possible for formal reasons. Widening the training of judicial professionals could help. It would be wise to consider including courses in EU criminal law and judicial cooperation instruments in the basic training for judicial authorities. From another perspective, this situation should be borne in mind when developing new instruments for judicial cooperation in the EU. They should be easy to use for both specialist experts and all other judicial authorities who may be confronted with judicial cooperation.

Another interesting observation concerns the internal organisation of law enforcement and judicial authorities in some Member States. Particularly in the case of the transfer of criminal proceedings, it appears that in some Member States, for reasons of internal organisation (sometimes related to formal elements of criminal procedure),[13] it is difficult to process requests and ensure their execution. We feel that this situation demands acknowledgement and attention at EU level, as is the case in the framework of the Mutual evaluation cycles. It should be addressed in a constructive manner, without naming and shaming. If it is not addressed properly, there is a real

12 See EJN Conclusions October 2021, *Hearing by Videoconference without the involvement of the Executing Member State.*

13 For example, after a transfer of proceedings, further investigation and prosecution in the executing Member States requires the opening of a special inquiry before an investigating judge, who may be reluctant to investigate the case.

risk that a future new instrument aiming to improve the transfer of criminal proceedings between Member States creates a paper reality.

Finally, we must be aware of the differences that exist in the financing of the criminal justice system in individual Member States. Those differences may affect the possibilities of judicial authorities to cooperate with their counterparts in other Member States. A good example are the costs of translation in the framework of the transfer of proceedings. Some judicial authorities interviewed in the course of our project explained that they are not responsible for those costs (which are borne by other governmental institutions), some of them have large budgets to cover those costs, while other judicial authorities have to pay them from a limited budget. The latter situation may, of course, act as a negative incentive for engaging in a procedure for the transfer of proceedings. In a sense, there is therefore a financial bias in the judicial cooperation in the EU.

2.4 Technological development

Technological innovation can be a great asset to the judicial cooperation in the European Union. We can think of the broad availability of videoconferencing facilities, a secured intranet that facilitates swift communication between the authorities of Member States, integrated translation tools and virtual databases on suspects who are the subject of ongoing investigations in Member States which could be consulted by judicial authorities on a hit/no hit basis.

All these examples would endorse and significantly improve the judicial cooperation in criminal matters between Member States. The European Commission is acting upon this assumption. In 2020, a report on Cross-border Digital Criminal Justice was published based on an analysis by Deloitte.[14] For all the subjects mentioned above, initiatives have been taken, which are now in different stages of realisation.[15] Some might prove to be more challenging than others. Think of the virtual database containing information on ongoing investigations: there are profound concerns about the possible risks for the confidentiality of investigations that such a tool might create. However, practitioners are striving to create a working solution.[16] Overall, technical innovation may be a game changer for the judicial cooperation in the European Union.

14 See Deloitte, Cross-border Digital Criminal Justice; Final Report, European Commission, June 2020.

15 See Communication from the Commission, Digitalisation of justice in the European Union; A toolbox of opportunities, COM(2020)710 final.

16 The Bureau BES conducts f.e. a pilot (CIDaR) on possible matching of data to prevent parallel investigations.

2.5 The EU policy on security

Since 2015, the European Union has had a policy for security in place: the European Agenda on Security.[17] In 2020, it was updated by the communication on the EU Security Union Strategy.[18] This provides a basis for coordinating the efforts of law enforcement authorities of the Member States, as well as Europol and Eurojust. The agenda is supplemented by more detailed policy initiatives laid down in other documents.

Our project brings forth two different considerations regarding the EU policy on security.

Firstly, we feel that good use of judicial cooperation can play a significant role in combatting crime in the EU. In the Agenda on Security, judicial cooperation is mentioned, among other things with regard to the coordination of Eurojust and to technical innovation.[19] Little to no attention is paid to the extent to which judicial cooperation could help achieve particular goals in combatting specific forms of crime and what should be done to endorse this. On the other hand, the prevention of impunity is cited in the European Commission's preparatory documents as one of the main reasons for considering a new EU instrument on the transfer of criminal proceedings.[20] We feel that a well-functioning instrument for the transfer of criminal proceedings could indeed enhance the capacities of law enforcement to deal with criminal offences and cases with cross border elements. It expands the existing toolkit of EU legal instruments. But which tool can best be used, and its use promoted, to counter specific forms of crime? For both the effectiveness of criminal policy in the EU and for the guidance of practitioners in individual criminal cases, a clear vision is needed.

Secondly, during our interviews and other research activities, in particular one form of crime was often mentioned as a challenge for judicial authorities: minor Internet fraud, such as scams, committed in a cross-border context. These cases are frequent and there is a considerable risk that they remain unpunished. Authorities in the Member States are often uncertain which Member State should investigate these offences. And because of the minor damage in relation to the efforts that need to be taken to investigate the case, they may turn down single cases and rather wait until a pattern of fraud, involving the same suspects, is visible. Europol may not be the appropriate body to take on the challenge of these small cases, although it has

17 The European Agenda on Security, COM(2015) 185 final.

18 COM (2020) 605.

19 COM (2020) 605, p. 22.

20 See European Commission, Call for evidence for an impact assessment; Judicial cooperation in criminal matters – transfer of proceedings (common rules), Ref. Ares(2021)7026778.

stepped up its activity in the case of organized Internet fraud.[21] It also hosts an Internet page with links to local police organisations.[22]

EU citizens have legitimate expectations on what the European Union should bring them in terms of security. One should not underestimate the irritations of minor cases of Internet fraud for citizens across the EU. A coordinated response at EU level might be needed, starting with a proper assessment of the extent of the problem.

21 Europol EC3 European Cybercrime Center, https://www.europol.europa.eu/about-europol/european-cybercrime-centre-ec3.

22 https://www.europol.europa.eu/report-a-crime/report-cybercrime-online.

3 The transfer of criminal proceedings: the current state of play

3.1 Introduction

We conducted empirical research into the current practice of the transfer of criminal proceedings between Member States of the EU. The practice shows that there are different types of situations and circumstances that inspire judicial authorities to issue a request for transfer of criminal proceedings. These types of situations and circumstances consist of a combination of different sorts of criminal offences, of elements constituting criteria for considering a transfer and of the specific stage of the investigations or prosecution of those criminal offences. Although this could potentially lead to a seemingly endless number of different examples, we can categorise and set out some typical situations where a transfer of proceedings is considered and performed.

It should be noted that a transfer of criminal proceedings is possible for every criminal offence, whether or not a suspect has already been identified. When a suspect has been identified, depending on the stage of the proceedings, and according to the national law of the Member States involved, they may be either referred to as a suspect or an accused person.

The (request for) transfer of proceedings requires a legal basis. Depending on which instruments Member States are a party, two or three (sometimes even more[23]) legal instruments may serve as a legal basis to effectuate a transfer.[24] These legal instruments each bring their own characteristics, and effect on their turn the practice of the transfer of criminal proceedings.

23 Some Member States have bilateral or multilateral regional instruments in place that may serve as a basis for the transfer of criminal proceedings. Examples of these instruments include the Nordic Cooperation Agreement between Finland, Norway, Sweden, Iceland and Denmark and an agreement between Poland, Slovakia, Czech Republic, Lithuania, and Ukraine.

24 It should be noted that the domestic law of Member States sometimes allows a transfer of proceedings without any international legal basis.

Judicial authorities often link the transfer of criminal proceedings to the subject of conflicts of jurisdiction. What exactly is the relation between these two subjects? We will elaborate on this question, based on the findings of our research.

Finally, we became aware of the big influence that the basis for prosecution in the domestic law of the Member States – the question whether prosecution is based on the principle of legality or the opportunity principle – considerably affects the way in which their judicial authorities look at the transfer of proceedings. It determines their possibilities to use the transfer of criminal proceedings as a tool, it defines their considerations to use it and shapes their expectations with regard to the procedure that should be followed by the executing Member State.

3.2 Statistical information

Introduction

As an element of our empirical research, we asked the authorities of the participating Member States if they could share statistical information about the use of transfer of proceedings. We were primarily interested in the number of incoming and outgoing requests. Furthermore, we would have been interested in information about the content of the cases that were the subject of a transfer of proceedings and possibly the delays of the decision-making process on accepting a request.

The availability of statistics turns out to be very limited. Information on numbers of incoming and outgoing requests is not complete, and information on the content of the cases concerned is nearly non-existent.

The reason often cited is that transfer of proceedings can take place directly between judicial authorities based on Article 21 of the 1959 Convention and Article 6 of the 2000 EU Convention on mutual assistance in criminal matters. This reduces the possibility for central authorities and Ministries of Justice to monitor the incoming and outgoing requests for a transfer of proceedings.

Some Member States could not reproduce any figures at all, others manually counted the number of requests coming in and going out in a number of districts. Other Member States gave a rough estimate. Only a few Member States have a database in place dedicated to judicial cooperation, where incoming and outgoing transfers of proceedings are registered alongside EIOs, transfers etc. are processed and monitored. EU instruments such as the Council Framework Decision on the European Arrest Warrant (EAW) and the Directive on the European Investigation Order do not oblige Member States to provide statistics about the use of those instruments in practice. However, from the moment of its entry into force, information on the use of EAWs has been collected and published on a yearly basis.[25]

In addition, it is generally not possible for Member States to establish which legal instrument served for the registered requests. Only statistics provided by Poland enable us to determine the basis on which the transfer took place (at least in how many cases a transfer took place and in how many of these cases the basis was found in Article 21 of the 1959 Convention).

Statistics provided do not include cases where proceedings were transferred in a more informal way, for example based on spontaneous exchange of information.

Although many indicated a need for this, also no figures exist on the follow up or the outcome of the specific cases.

Finally, it should be noted that even where a more comprehensive and dedicated database appears to exist, registered statistics by different Member States do not always seem to correspond to each other and therefore numbers of incoming and outgoing (formally registered) requests do not always match.

We can consider the absence of statistical information as a handicap for our research project. In a broader context, the absence of data on different modalities of judicial cooperation presents a significant shortcoming in the assessment of the acquis. Concrete numbers and information can help to understand the functioning of the legal framework, and to determine the relation between the different instruments of the legal framework.

Nevertheless, we can draw some general conclusions from the received data.

Statistical data collected

From the statistics received from the nine Member States participating in our research project, it seems that these Member States generally receive more requests for transfer of criminal proceedings than they issue. For example, Sweden and Poland seem to receive about two or three times more requests than they issue. Some Member States present statistics indicating a larger difference of four to five times as many incoming as outgoing requests, for example Romania. From the figures received, the differences seem to be biggest in the Netherlands with a difference of more than twenty times as many incoming as outgoing requests for transfer of criminal proceedings.

25 Currently based on the questionnaire set out in doc. 11356/13. Information is provided on a voluntary basis by the Member States to the European Commission.

Austria seems to be an exception to this observation, sending out more requests than it receives. It also presents an enormous total of requests. While neither of these numbers is restricted to EU Member States, Austria, for example, indicates that it will issue more than 1900 requests in 2018, while indicating that it received just under 500 requests that year.

Although Belgium could not provide figures for the period 2018-2020, data received from other Member States seem to indicate that Belgium generally sends out more requests to Member States than it receives from the same Member States. At the same time, it should be noted again that these figures only include formal registered data. Informal transfers via spontaneous exchange of information have not been registered.

The statistics show that, in general, most requests for a transfer of criminal proceedings seem to be made between neighbouring Member States. This was also confirmed during the on-site interviews. Some neighbouring Member States have an alternative basis for the transfer of criminal proceedings in multilateral treaties they have in place. Such is the case for the Nordic states as well as the Baltic states and some Eastern Europe states.[26] It also emerged from the interviews that the existence of these separate agreements may also explain the more frequent transfers between the parties to these agreements now that there is often a simplified or clearer arrangement with regard to the procedure, the translation of documents and costs. Member States using those regional instruments tend to have a better idea about who to contact and have access to extensive knowledge of each other's criminal law systems.

3.3 Types of cases and criteria at stake

Based on our analysis, we can distinguish three different categories of cases where a transfer of proceedings under the current practice is considered and performed. Other distinctions between categories of cases would also have been possible. However, we feel that the distinction chosen is the most helpful in our analysis. We made sure we received feedback on this distinction in the different phases of our research project, and the distinction was subsequently adjusted and confirmed.

Each category has its own criteria to consider the transfer of proceedings, and requirements regarding the materialisation of the transfer.

26 See supra note 22.

Category I: (Transborder) organized crime

Category I consists of cases of organized crime that are often a committed in a transborder context. But it also possible that the transborder element is not provided by the offences themselves, but by the perpetrators involved.

Examples include ATM bombings, drug-related crime, human trafficking and other forms of organized crime.

There might be several different criteria at stake that indicate a transfer of proceedings. Think of the location of evidence (the Member State where the core of the investigations has taken place) or possible other (connected) proceedings. The nationality or place of residence of suspects, the possibility that the suspect already faces prosecution for other criminal offences in another Member State, or that the suspect is already serving a prison sentence in another Member State may also play a role, but perhaps to a lesser extent. In contrast to this, the nationality or residence of victims is not often cited as a reason.

It is also in these organized crime cases that investigations may be conducted by a Joint investigation team (JIT) and that there may be involvement of Eurojust: either in the setting up of the JIT and/or in coordinating the prosecutorial efforts.

The main challenge that respondents indicate especially with regard to Category I offences is the timely identification of such cases. Transborder crime triggers the attention of law enforcement authorities of Member States concerned. Independently of each other, parallel investigations may be opened in several Member States. There is no warning mechanism that prevents these parallel investigations of which authorities are unaware. Respondents in our research project stated that the Council Framework Decision on conflicts of jurisdiction (2009/948/JHA) is of little help. Other areas of concern are common to the transfer of proceedings, such as elevated costs of a transfer due to translation of files or a lack of feedback about the outcome of the proceedings in the receiving Member State after the case has been transferred. The compatibility of evidence is also mentioned. One particular concern relates to the court proceedings that take place in the receiving Member State after the taking over of the file. The strict application of the principle of immediacy which governs court proceedings in the criminal procedure of many Member States might have as an effect that witnesses residing in the receiving Member State have to testify, including undercover police officers. Some Member States are reluctant to expose their officers to this.

Category II: Cases of 'ordinary' crime with a transborder aspect

This category may include all kinds of different offences. We could say that it basically includes all offences that do not qualify for Category I or Category III. Typical examples are cases of online fraud or dissemination of child pornography where the suspect is acting from the territory of another Member State, and theft committed by suspects residing in another Member State. Other types of cases are those of tourists perpetrating offences such as destroying objects, committing public violence and theft, whilst on holiday in another Member State. The suspects concerned have often already returned to the Member State of residence before the investigations are concluded, except for cases in which they have been taken into pre-trial detention.

More exceptionally, it may concern very serious criminal offences. Prosecution of these cases tends to be fixed to where the crime was committed. The big social impact of such crimes may be a negative indication for a transfer of proceedings. However, there are examples of such cases that were subject of a transfer of proceedings. One of those examples is the manslaughter committed by a Dutchman on another Dutchman during a holiday in Spain – in the Netherlands referred to as 'the Mallorca case'.[27] In the early hours of 14 July 2021, two groups of Dutch youngsters on holiday in Mallorca got into a street fight with each other, resulting in the death of a 27-year-old. After some preliminary investigations, the Spanish authorities decided to request a transfer of the case to the Netherlands, where the investigations were continued and at present court proceedings are underway for manslaughter and attempted manslaughter.[28]

Criteria that indicate a possible request for the transfer of proceedings differ from one case to another and cover the whole list of criteria set out in instruments such as the European Convention for the Transfer of Criminal Proceedings.[29] Quite often, a combination of several criteria is applicable. The main criteria are that the suspect resides in another Member State, or that the main part of the offence was committed in another Member State or evidence is most likely to be found in that other state. The position of victims is also referred to as an important criterion, but with a complementary character only (it is not a main criterion).

Challenges from the perspective of the requesting authorities cited in the interviews, concern mostly the willingness of the receiving Member State to take over the case, and the costs related to translation of the file. A lack of feedback about the decision on the request and the follow-up after a transfer has taken place, is mentioned as well. Challenges experienced from the perspective of receiving authorities, include the lack of justification as to why they would be in a better position to pursue the case, the absence of translation of supporting documents, no prior consultation to exchange views on the desirability of a transfer, and premature requests. Examples of the latter include cases wherein the requesting authority failed to perform some

27 https://www.eur.nl/en/news/dutch-prosecution-fatal-abuse-case-mallorca.

28 This case also provides an example of two Member States that are both a party to the 1972 Convention but use Article 21 of the 1959 Convention to perform the transfer of proceedings.

29 See Article 8, par. 1.

additional inquiries in the case, allowing it to conclude that the receiving Member State was not in the best position to take over the prosecution, or cases where, after a transfer of proceedings, additional investigations prove necessary in the requesting Member State forcing the authorities to file EIOs.

Category III: Small offences in border regions

The contours of a third category emerged in several interviews, in part overlapping with the previous category with regard to the type of offence, but distinct with regard to the region in which they take place. Daily life in border regions in the EU is so intermingled that residents of different Member States often cross borders several times a day to go to work, visit family or to go shopping. This leads to many situations in which small offences are committed on either side of the border.

Examples include a resident from Member State A who hits a pole in the parking lot of a supermarket in Member State B and returns home. Or a couple from Member State C that gets into a marital dispute while visiting a restaurant in Member State D. The authorities from Member States B and D will be inclined to merely inform the authorities of Member States A and C of the destruction of state property and of the violent altercation rather than making an official request for a transfer of proceedings. The information may be transmitted at a police level or between judicial authorities. In the latter case, it can be considered a spontaneous exchange of information, based on Article 7 of the EU Convention on mutual legal assistance.

There are several reasons why a formal request for a transfer of proceedings is deemed inappropriate in these cases. Firstly, authorities are quite often reluctant to initiate official inquiries in these cases, so technically there are not yet proceedings that could be subject of a transfer. A second reason is that the aim of the authorities is merely to inform the authorities of the other Member State, so they do not necessarily require any follow up from those authorities or reporting back.

Experts interviewed on this topic expressed their desire to keep the possibility of dealing with this category of cases by simply performing an exchange of information. In their opinion, a new legal instrument should leave room for this. It should not make things more difficult in practice.

3.4 The existing European legal framework

The 1972 Convention on Transfer of Proceedings and Article 21 of the 1959 Convention on Mutual Assistance

One of the reasons for this research project, was the inconsistency of the legal framework for transfer of proceedings in criminal matters in the EU. There is a specific

European instrument on the transfer of criminal proceedings: the Council of Europe European Convention on the Transfer of Proceedings in Criminal Matters (1972).[30] 13 of the EU Member States ratified this convention: Austria, Bulgaria, Cyprus, the Czech Republic, Denmark, Estonia, Latvia, Lithuania, the Netherlands, Romania, the Slovak Republic, Spain and Sweden.

This means that another 14 Member States must rely on the second legal basis for the transfer of criminal proceedings: Article 21 of the Council of Europe Convention of Mutual Assistance in Criminal Matters (1959).[31] All Member States are a party to the 1959 Convention as, so this instrument enables a transfer of criminal proceedings to be performed EU wide.

There is a big difference between these legal bases for the transfer of criminal proceedings. The 1972 Convention is a dedicated instrument that offers a complete step by step procedure for requesting a transfer of proceedings and a list of criteria that may support a transfer of proceedings. It also provides procedural rules for the decision on a request, including applicable grounds for refusal, and determines the effects of an accepted request of transfer of proceedings for both the issuing state and the receiving state.

Compared to the 1972 Convention, Article 21 of the 1959 Convention offers a very meagre regime for the transfer of criminal proceedings. It simply states:

1. *Information laid by one Contracting Party with a view to proceedings in the courts of another Party shall be transmitted between the Ministries of Justice concerned (..)*
2. *The receiving Party shall notify the requesting Party of any action taken on such information and shall forward a copy of the record of any verdict pronounced. (..)*

Technically speaking, Article 21 offers a possibility for an official 'denunciation' of a criminal offence. There is no obligation, no procedure. This results in an open context, giving little guidance to judicial authorities looking for any certainty about what to do and what to expect.

The particular situation of Member States that can use the two regimes because they are a party to both conventions demands our attention. One might assume that there is a hierarchy between the basic possibility of Article 21 of the 1959 Convention and the 1972 Convention. However, that is not the case.[32] In our research, we saw that Member States take a different position in this. Some oblige their authorities to use the 1972 Convention where possible, while others do not. This may lead to

30 CETS no. 073.
31 CETS no. 030.
32 Article 43 of the 1972 Convention does not exclude the use of Article 21 of the 1959 Convention between States that are both parties to the 1972 Convention.

situations where national legislation implemented for the 1972 Convention is used to perform a transfer based on Article 21 of the 1959 Convention, for example. To be clear: there is no harm in this, but it is remarkable.

Paradoxically, some experts tend to see the thin basis of Article 21 of the 1959 Convention as providing the preferred and modern instrument for judicial cooperation with respect to the transfer of proceedings compared to the 1972 Convention. In fact, Article 6 of the EU Convention on mutual legal assistance states that judicial authorities can send requests based on Article 21 of the 1959 Convention directly to the judicial authorities of another Member State.[33] On the other hand, the 1972 Convention still prescribes the transmission of requests for the transfer of criminal proceedings between Ministries of Justice. Another perceived advantage is the flexibility that Article 21 of the 1959 Convention offers. Article 21 leaves it entirely to the discretion of the receiving judicial authority to accept or refuse a request for the transfer of proceedings, unlike the 1972 Convention which provides a detailed procedure for the receiving Member State how to assess a request.

Article 7 of the 2000 EU Convention

In the previous paragraph, we came across another legal basis that might be used in situations where judicial authorities want to refer possible investigations or prosecution to another Member State: the spontaneous exchange of information. Article 7, paragraph 1, of the EU Convention on mutual legal assistance provides a legal basis:[34]

> 1. *Within the limits of their national law, the competent authorities of the Member States may exchange information, without a request to that effect, relating to criminal offences and the infringements of rules of law referred to in Article 3(1), the punishment or handling of which falls within the competence of the receiving authority at the time the information is provided. (..)*

There is a significant difference on what role this modality may fulfil in practice, depending on the prosecutorial system that a Member State has in place. Judicial authorities that are bound by the legality principle might need a formal decision to dispose of a case when a criminal offence has been established. In these legal systems, a spontaneous exchange of information does not allow the judicial authority to subsequently stop the procedure.

33 This possibility can also be concluded from Article 4 of the Second Additional Protocol to the European Convention on the Mutual Assistance in Criminal Matters (2001), CETS no. 182.

34 2000/C 197/01.

3.5 The stage of the investigation/prosecution where a transfer is considered

Another result of our empirical study is that the point in time at which a transfer of proceedings is usually considered varies.

A reasonably clear assessment is possible for the investigation and prosecution of organized crime (Category I cases). If the proceedings concern an organized crime case, the investigations are usually at an advanced stage or have even been terminated when a request for a transfer of proceedings is made.

The situation is different with respect to small offences in border regions (Category III cases). There, a request – or rather a spontaneous exchange of information – is usually performed at the beginning of the investigation or even before any investigation has been initiated.

Similarly, unambiguous statements cannot be made with regard to cases of ordinary criminality (Category II cases). Here, the moment when the transfer of the case is considered varies enormously. In a future regulation, a strong requirement should be that the issuing Member State has conducted some investigations and, based on the outcome, can motivate and justify why the other Member State is in a better position to prosecute. In other instances, a spontaneous exchange of information is the preferred option.

Figure 3 Moment of the transfer of the case

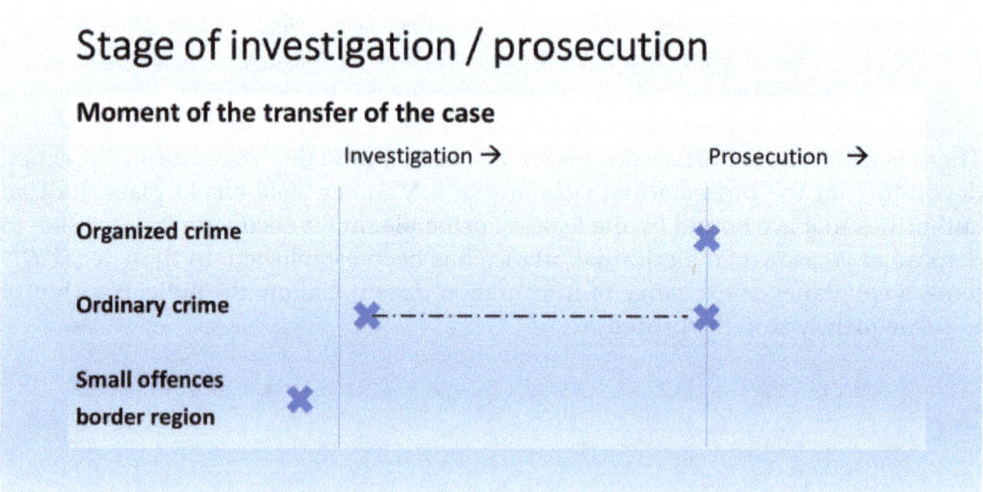

3.6 Conflicts of jurisdiction

In the answers to our questionnaire and during the interviews, the subject of conflicts of jurisdiction was often raised. It was sometimes presented as the underlying problem in the judicial cooperation, to which the transfer of criminal proceedings tries to provide a solution.

There are indeed multiple relations between the topics of conflicts of jurisdiction and the transfer of criminal proceedings.[35] But we need to clearly distinguish between the topics as an issue in the practice of law enforcement in the EU (conflicts of jurisdiction) and a modality of judicial cooperation (the transfer of criminal proceedings). The Council Framework Decision 2008/948/JHA on the prevention and settlement of conflicts of exercise of jurisdiction in criminal proceedings should lay a bridge between the two topics.

Council Framework Decision 2008/948/JHA

Article 5 of Council Framework Decision 2008/948/JHA prescribes contact between Member States in case of possible parallel procedures. This has basically two aims: to prevent bis in idem situations and to determine which Member State should preferably continue the proceedings.[36] The mandatory notice shall contain different types of information about the case (Article 8). In all instances where parallel investigations have been established following this notice, the judicial authorities concerned are obliged to enter into direct consultations 'in order to reach consensus on any effective solution aimed at avoiding the adverse consequences arising from such parallel proceedings, which may, where appropriate, lead to the concentration of the criminal proceedings in one Member State' (Article 10). The Council Framework Decision does not specify what criteria may be used as an argument to refer further prosecution to one or the other Member State. Relevant criteria are mentioned in the Eurojust Guidelines for deciding 'Which jurisdiction should prosecute?';[37] these criteria are very similar to the criteria used when judicial authorities consider a request for the transfer of proceedings.

As a matter of fact, the outcome of the consultation may be that it is best to transfer proceedings from one Member State to another Member State. But this is not always necessary: one of the Member States can also decide to stop the proceedings and to

35 See f.e. M. Carmona Ruano, Prevention and settlement of conflicts of jurisdiction (Spanish system), in: K. Ligeti e.al. (eds), *Preventing and resolving conflicts of jurisdiction in EU Criminal Law*, Oxford: Oxford University Press 2018, p. 119-139; M. Kaiafa-Gbandi, Addressing the Problems of Jurisdictional Conflicts in Criminal Matters within the EU, *EUCRIM* 2020, no. 3, p. 209-212.

36 See Article 1.

37 Eurojust, Guidelines for deciding 'Which jurisdiction should prosecute?', revised version 2016, p. 3-4.

hand over relevant information (for example based on an EIO or as a spontaneous exchange of information) to the other Member State.

In several interviews, respondents stressed their opinion that Council Framework Decision 2008/948/JHA is not working properly. The exchange of information is performed at random and covers only a part of potential parallel investigations.[38] It creates a level of uncertainty in the investigation of transborder crime and inefficiency in law enforcement and consequently prevents an effective use of the transfer of criminal proceedings.

3.7 The influence of the legality principle or opportunity principle

In the course of our research, we gained the impression that there is a strong difference in the way Member States look at the transfer of criminal proceedings, what is their mindset, depending on the principle that governs their decision to prosecute. There are fundamental differences here between Member States where the legality principle is the starting point for prosecution and Member States where the opportunity principle applies from the outset.

According to the legality principle, the prosecuting authorities must act *ex officio*, even in the absence of a complaint, when they suspect a criminal offence. The principle of opportunity, on the other hand, leaves the decision to act with regard to a specific offence to the discretion of the public prosecutor. It is important to note, though, that these principles are not implemented in pure form; especially the legality principle can be subject to (more or less far reaching) exceptions.[39] Among the Member States involved in our project, the opportunity principle is applied in Belgium, France and the Netherlands, whereas Germany, Austria, Romania, Spain and Sweden apply the legality principle.

The way the aforementioned principles operate in different Member States influences the request for a transfer of proceedings as well as the decision on this request. In addition, these principles play a role in the acceptance of different settlement modalities, wishes with regard to communication about the follow-up after a transfer and the final outcome of the case, etc. The different ways in which the principles work in different Member States mean that different Member States sometimes have

38 It can be noted that the Directive on combatting terrorism (2017/541/EU) in its Article 22 – amending Decision 2005/671/JHA – gives an obligation to share information regarding terrorist offences 'where the information could be used in the prevention, detection, investigation or prosecution of terrorist offences'. This provision offers by its more concrete wording and because of addressing one specific (very serious) form of crime, probably a better working alternative.

39 For the situation in Germany, see M. Bohlander, *Principles of German Criminal Procedure*, 2012, p. 25-27.

different grounds for a transfer and different Member States require different formalities. On a more abstract level, this gives the impression that the activities of law enforcement agencies are influenced by different 'cultures of prosecution'. In practice, this creates ambiguities and divergent 'practices' between countries.

In general, Member States in which the prosecution of criminal offences is governed by the legality principle will typically use a dedicated instrument to transfer proceedings. The reasons for this are that they want certainty about the case being pursued and that they need confirmation about the outcome to officially terminate their own prosecution of the case. Member States for whom the opportunity principle applies enjoy more flexibility in their choice of an instrument. They will often prefer a dedicated instrument that provides guidance. But they also have the possibility to use the informal way to transfer the proceedings to another Member State. For example, they can – after agreed parallel investigations – simply stop the case and use an EIO or perform a spontaneous exchange of information to put the judicial authority of another Member State in position to continue the prosecution.

While for prosecutors whose activities are subject to the legality principle, a request for a transfer of proceedings is a means to fulfil their duty to prosecute. Due to their discretionary power, public prosecutors acting on the basis of the opportunity principle always have the possibility to abstain from (further) prosecution when they consider that prosecution in another Member State would be the better option, but have the overall feeling that there is too little interest to pursue the case and therefore simply decide to stop it and drop charges. And while the prosecutor who is required to observe the legality principle will expect some guarantee of prosecution by the executing Member State, his colleague who is given more freedom by the opportunity principle usually needs this confirmation only in high profile cases.

Moreover, traces of the two different 'cultures of prosecution' can also be found in the decision on the acceptance of a request: under the application of the principle of opportunity, public prosecutors are usually used to having room to consider the merits of the case when deciding whether to start prosecution and will not abstain from this when they find themselves confronted with a request to take over proceedings. Prosecutors required to follow the legality principle will feel more bound here.

Once the proceedings have been taken over, the legality principle creates a general obligation to prosecute (with only limited exceptions). If the formal requirements are met, there is mostly no formal reason to drop charges. By contrast, under the application of the opportunity principle, there is a broader possibility to drop charges even after the decision to take over. And finally, as mentioned above, the requirements of the legality principle make it necessary for the requesting prosecutor to receive feedback about the outcome to be able to officially close the case. When applying the opportunity principle, on the contrary, feedback may be appreciated in general but is required only in high profile cases.

3.8 Conclusion

The outcome of this chapter can be brought together in the following diagram:

Figure 4 The legal and practical context of the different kinds of cases combined

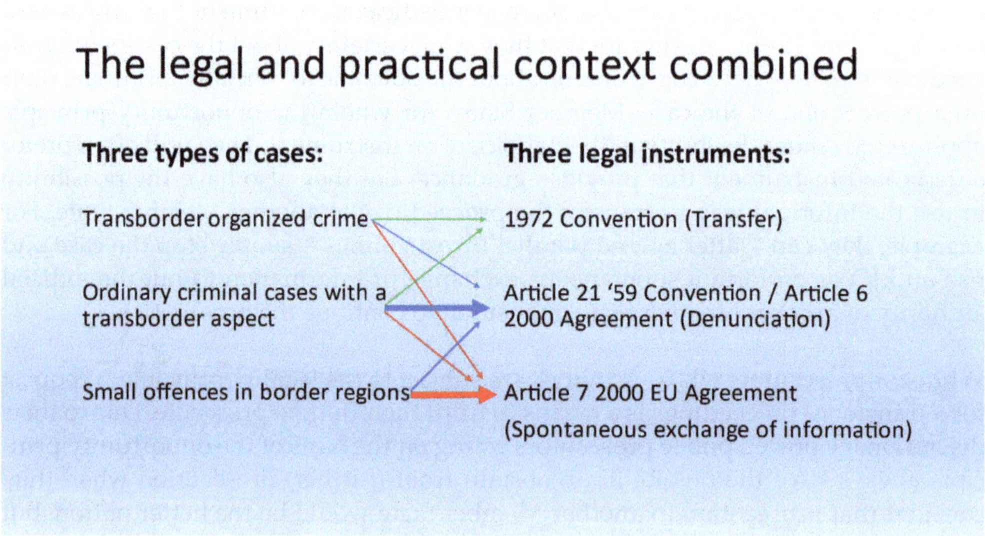

Explanation

In cases of Trans border organized crime (Category I), we can observe the use of all three legal modalities to achieve the transfer of further prosecution to another Member State. The thin blue line indicates the use of Article 21 of the 1959 Convention, the thin green line indicates the use of the 1972 Convention and the thin red line the use of the spontaneous exchange of information based on Article 7 of the 2000 EU Convention. The latter is possible for Member States that have the opportunity principle as a basis for prosecution.

The thick blue line (indicating a suspected large number of cases) points to the use of the Article 21 1959 basis as the main solution in Category II cases. Other possibilities include the use of the 1972 Convention (thin green line) or spontaneous exchange of information (thin red line) in the case of Member States using the opportunity principle for their decision on prosecution.

The thick red line (pointing at a suspected large number of situations) concerns the use of the spontaneous exchange of information as a main solution in Category III cases.

4 Some impressions about the challenges in practice

4.1 Introduction

The extensive project work, which included thorough literature research as well as the application of various empirical instruments, brought us into contact with a large number of problems that practitioners encounter with regard to a transfer of proceedings in criminal matters. When these problems are discussed in some detail below, this certainly is not aimed at overly criticising the existing practice or articulating fundamental reservations against a transfer of proceedings. On the contrary, the project consortium is naturally committed to finding constructive solutions regarding the topic that is in its focus. However, the development of convincing solutions requires an in-depth analysis of the status quo (with all its problematic implications). It is only on the basis of an honest examination of legal reality that sound proposals for its improvement can be developed.

4.2 Stumbling blocks on a practical level

One of the basic findings of our research is that clear rules on the practical and organisational level are so far lacking. In our empirical work – in particular the on-site interviews – and in the discussions at the two Working Conferences, various questions were repeatedly articulated that relate to the operational implementation of a transfer of proceedings:

- In which situations should a request for transfer of proceedings be considered?
- Should there be a prior consultation between judicial authorities of the Member States concerned?
- At which stage of the investigations can a transfer of proceedings best take place?
- What information is needed to motivate and substantiate a request?
- Which information and parts of the file should be translated, who should take care of the translation and which Member State should bear the costs for the translation?

The frequency and urgency with which these and related issues were raised in the course of the interviews and conferences suggest that the creation of a reliable and transparent operational framework is one of the key challenges to be addressed by a future instrument on the transfer of proceedings.

Another finding is that clear criteria for determining where prosecution could best take place in the interest of a proper administration of justice are lacking so far. Some criteria are dominant, for example the nationality and residence of the suspect, and the place where the offence was committed. Another thing worth mentioning is that Member States often summarise the criteria as determining 'which Member State is in the best position to prosecute'. Although this phrase is undoubtedly somewhat vague, it truly emphasises the judicial cooperation element.

As regards the translation of the request for a transfer of proceedings and of the case file, we came across major differences in practice. Some Member States take care of all the translation (sometimes in their role as issuing Member State, sometimes in their role as executing Member State), while others are reluctant to do more than strictly necessary. Two challenges in particular arose in this context: the quality of the translation and – especially – the costs of translations. However, the cost aspect also requires a differentiated consideration: for some Member States costs related to translation are not an issue, for others they are. Our impression is that especially public prosecutors from Member States, whose work is governed by the legality principle, find it easier to justify even considerable translation costs than their colleagues for whom the opportunity principle applies. While the former can simply point to their obligation to prosecute, the latter seem more accustomed to making proportionality considerations with regard to spending their budget.

Another deficit that was frequently mentioned is that there is no European database on investigations and prosecution. This results in a lack of information about ongoing cases in other Member States concerning the same suspects or same offences. We see that there are developments or at least discussions regarding this aspect on a European level,[40] but the deficit character of the current situation should be taken into account when discussing the practical aspects of a transfer of proceedings.

We also came across difficulties regarding the coordination of provisional measures already taken by the transferring Member State. The seizure of objects, etc. must be physically or virtually included in the transfer of criminal proceedings and there seems to be uncertainty as to how this should be done in individual cases. In the case of the freezing of proceeds of crime, a distinct procedure for money laundering, remaining in the issuing Member State seems to be an alternative to a transfer.

---

40 See Deloitte, Cross-border Digital Criminal Justice; Final Report, European Commission, June 2020.

Under certain circumstances, problems may also arise regarding the use of evidence: evidence collected in the issuing Member State can mostly be used in the executing Member State without problems, but this is subject to some exceptions, notably if the evidence or investigative method could not be used in domestic cases in the executing Member State.

Another problem is that so far there is no duty to follow up on a request for transfer of proceedings (and thus no time limit regarding the communication on it). Experts have pointed to a lack of communication about the reception of the request, about the decision to take over, about the follow up to be provided by the executing Member State and what could (tentatively) be expected about the outcome. This can result in a notorious lack of information in the transferring Member State which can be of particular relevance for those Member States in which the prosecution of criminal offences is governed by the principle of legality, where the public prosecutor needs to know about the outcome of the further proceedings to be able to close the case.

4.3 Challenges of a more fundamental nature

In the course of our research, we also encountered several issues that are of a more fundamental nature. They touch on key questions of the transfer of proceedings and are therefore likely to generate intensive discussions when the contours of a dedicated instrument are negotiated.

Jurisdiction

A particularly delicate issue is the question of subsidiary or complementary jurisdiction which could be regulated in a new instrument. The possible absence of jurisdiction did not come up as a primary concern in the interviews. We had the impression that a possible lack in jurisdiction is not felt as a gap in the framework for the transfer of criminal proceedings.

In our interviews, most experts and representatives of Member States did mention a possible lack of jurisdiction as a primary concern in the case of the transfer of proceedings. At the same time, they did not oppose the prospect of an extra basis for jurisdiction. However, it must be remembered that a proposal to create complementary jurisdiction led to fierce discussions during the last attempt to create a dedicated instrument for the transfer of proceedings in 2009.[41] In addition, there is a lack of binding rules on how to deal with jurisdiction conflicts, which is relevant,

41 See B. de Jonge, *Transfer of criminal proceedings: from stumbling block to cornerstone of cooperation in criminal matters in the EU*, ERA Forum 2020, 449 (p. 455-456).

among other things, for a proper application of the ne bis in idem principle. The Europe-wide database that was just mentioned (see 4.2) could be useful here.

Fundamental rights

Another important issue in the context discussed here is fundamental rights. Several interviews were conducted with defence lawyers specialised in trans-border cases. In these interviews, certain fundamental rights issues were addressed which should also be kept in mind when contemplating a dedicated instrument. For example, the question arises whether the EAW is a viable alternative to a transfer of proceedings: in other words, should a transfer of proceedings, given its far less intrusive effects for the suspect, not be the promoted solution when possible?

Irritation can be caused by different levels of sanctions in different Member States and in this context, the applicability of the *lex mitior* principle can be an issue. Furthermore, the role of the suspect and of the victim in a transfer of proceedings must be clarified and there must be sufficient safeguards for both the rights of the suspect and the rights of the victim.

Mutual recognition

Furthermore, the implications of the principle of mutual recognition for a transfer of proceedings need clarification. As a matter of fact, the EU legal framework for the judicial cooperation in criminal matters is built on the principle of mutual recognition. When applied to the transfer of criminal proceedings, this principle could cause a real paradigm shift compared to the current practice which is mainly built on an open ended and non-binding instrument (Article 21 of the 1959 Council of Europe Convention on mutual legal assistance).

Against this background, the question arises as to what the meaning of mutual recognition is (or should be) with respect to the transfer of criminal proceedings. Does it refer to the acceptance of establishment of the facts, the collected evidence etc., or does it also entail mandatory execution of the request by the receiving Member State (except in the case of grounds for refusal)? If the latter were the case, it would become even more important to have requirements in place for the motivation of the request by the issuing authority. Also, in the eyes of the authorities of Member States that use the opportunity principle as a basis for prosecution, such a mandatory execution of a request for transfer of proceedings would be a big exception to the way they normally appreciate – in domestic cases – the merits of a case before they decide to further investigate or prosecute it.

4.4 Lack of justification of requests

Finally, clarification is needed on how to deal with insufficiently substantiated requests to take over proceedings. For example, the question may arise as to how to respond when there is some reason to consider a transfer. However, there are also doubts as to whether the receiving Member State is really in a better position to prosecute than the issuing Member State and whether the case has been properly investigated in the issuing Member State. In practice, there still seems to be a lack of communication in this context. Often negative decisions are taken by the receiving Member State without prior consultation and only formally communicated to the issuing Member State. Instead of a unilateral refusal, follow-up investigations by the issuing Member State could be suggested and, if necessary, controversially discussed here. In any case, it should be avoided that the executing Member State feels compelled to pursue investigations in the issuing Member State (e.g., by EIOs etc.) after taking over the proceedings.

5 Proposed solutions: building blocks for a new legal instrument

5.1 Introduction

Improvement: facilitating the use of transfer of criminal proceedings

There is a broad consensus between experts, policy advisors and legislative lawyers that it is worthwhile trying to improve the transfer of criminal proceedings between Member States in the European Union. There are clearly opportunities to successfully address the challenges that are identified in the current practice.

That being said, certainly at the beginning of the project, when the announcement of the preparation of a proposal for a legal instrument by the European Commission had not yet been made, there were varying opinions among experts on the question whether a new legal instrument was the best way to improve the transfer of proceedings. Experts critical about a new legal instrument pointed to the possible loss of flexibility that a legal instrument could cause.

This fear about a loss of flexibility seems to have at least two different aspects. The first aspect leads us back to the introductory remarks at the beginning of this report: the ambiguous character of the current situation where the legal framework offers little hold for practitioners performing a transfer of proceedings. At the same time, this is perceived as both a problem and a blessing. A problem, because there is no certainty about the effect given to their request, and feedback is lacking. A blessing, because of the room available to judicial authorities receiving a request for a transfer of proceedings to weigh all kinds of consideration: such as limited available capacity for investigation and prosecution. This directs all attention to the possible binding element of the issuing of a request for a transfer of proceedings, as a consequence of the application of the principle of mutual recognition. We will elaborate this in paragraph 5.3.

A second aspect of the fear for a loss of flexibility is that some experts indicate that they are concerned that a new legal instrument would end up in unnecessary bureaucracy. Authorities do not want to be obliged to use the new legal instrument in situations (think of Category III cases) where they currently use other, more informal solutions. Another concern affects the certificate that may be prescribed to perform a transfer of proceedings. Some authorities expressed their disappointment about the – in their eyes – complicated EIO certificate.[42] They urge law makers to keep a certificate for the transfer of proceedings as simple as possible (see further paragraph 5.7).

The legislative perspective

Since work is in progress towards a dedicated EU legal instrument on the transfer of criminal proceedings, it is wise to frame our proposals for a solution to the challenges in the field of the transfer of proceedings as possible elements of future legislation. The solutions will need to be part of a legislative instrument: a regulation or a directive.

When considering solutions, we can benefit from the legislative perspective. Thinking of solutions from a legislative perspective shows that one can achieve results by describing a procedure step by step (this provides guidance). And that sometimes it is more effective to envisage a combination of small provisions that together work out fine, instead of setting out one binding and possibly controversial hard rule.

There is an example of how an EU instrument might look: the draft Council Framework Decision of 2009. We come to the conclusion that its content can be a good starting point for most of the topics that need to be addressed.

In the following paragraphs, we will propose solutions for the identified challenges, drafted as possible elements for future legislation. In a sense, they are building blocks.

5.2 The scope of the future legal instrument

There was a broad consensus among the respondents to the interviews and participants in the Working Conferences that a future legal instrument on the transfer of criminal proceedings should cover all offences, including minor ones. Within the legal framework for judicial cooperation in the EU, the transfer of proceedings is a tool that can be used in cases of petty crime and can prevent impunity. In those cases, the issuing of an EAW will not always be possible given the threshold set out in Article 2, paragraph 1, of the Council Framework Decision on the EAW: a

42 This is also reflected in Eurojust, *Report on Eurojust's casework in the field of the European Investigation Order*, November 2020, p. 52.

custodial sentence or a detention order for a maximum period of at least 12 months by the law of the issuing Member State is required.

Another important element regarding the scope of an instrument for the transfer of proceedings is that it should allow for the transfer of proceedings at every stage in the pre-trial phase: from the moment the investigation into the criminal offence has not yet started until the conclusion of the investigation and a decision on further prosecution is taken. Participants in the second Working Conference were of the opinion that a possibility to transfer proceedings should exist even during the trial phase, if the national law of the issuing Member State so provides.

It follows from our research that a new dedicated instrument on the transfer of proceedings should leave some room for alternative solutions. This takes into account the spontaneous exchange of information (based on Article 7 of the EU Convention on Mutual Legal Assistance), which can be an easy way forward in circumstances where a transfer of proceedings would also be possible. This provides flexibility. On the other hand, clear rules should be established on the relationship between the new legal instrument and other corresponding instruments. The legislator of the Directive on the EIO failed to do so, and that causes problems to this day.[43] We feel that, after adopting a new dedicated EU instrument on the transfer of proceedings in criminal matters, the application of both the 1972 Convention and Article 21 of the 1959 Convention should be excluded.[44]

5.3 Mutual recognition

Regulating the transfer of criminal proceedings as a tool within the legal framework for judicial cooperation in the European Union seems to presuppose an instrument that is based on the principle of mutual recognition. This can be derived from Article 82, paragraph 1, TFEU, that reads:

> *1. Judicial cooperation in criminal matters in the Union shall be based on the principle of mutual recognition of judgments and judicial decisions (..).*
>
> *The European Parliament and the Council, acting in accordance with the ordinary legislative procedure, shall adopt measures to:*
>
> *(a) lay down rules and procedures for ensuring recognition throughout the Union of all forms of judgments and judicial decisions (..)*

43 Eurojust, *Report on Eurojust's casework in the field of the European Investigation Order*, November 2020, p. 52.

44 See Article 21 of the draft Council Framework Decision that contains some rules about the relationship of the instrument with other agreements and arrangements.

But what does mutual recognition entail when applied to the transfer of proceedings in criminal matters?

During the interviews and in our first Working Conference in January 2022, participating experts expressed a clear preference for an instrument that was based on a request rather than an 'order'. An order, used in the framework of the Directive on the EIO, would imply mandatory execution. This was deemed undesirable. Several reasons were cited in this respect.

Firstly, there is a fear that authorities would be overwhelmed if there were an 'order' for a transfer of proceedings. Such an order could present a very simple way of getting rid of numbers of small, insignificant cases that would then land on the desk of judicial authorities in another Member State. Such a fear does not necessarily point to a lack of trust between judicial authorities. It is merely an observation that this could happen. The risk of overwhelming could be prevented by introducing targeted measures such as a threshold excluding minor offences, for example with a minimum punishment in the issuing and or executing Member State. Or by enhancing the requirements with regard to the criteria that may give rise to issuing an order for the transfer of proceedings. But looking at the current practice, such measures would exclude a number of cases where a transfer of proceedings provides a satisfactory solution. In turn, such preventive measures are undesirable.

A second more dogmatic argument was advanced and developed in a discussion among experts during the first Working Conference. They pointed to the difference between the transfer of proceedings and other forms of judicial cooperation, such as mutual legal assistance or extradition. In the latter forms of judicial cooperation, the executing Member State simply provides assistance to an ongoing criminal procedure in the issuing Member State, by executing an EIO or EAW.[45] It is the issuing Member State that bears responsibility for the content of that procedure and continues to do so after the judicial cooperation has taken place. This situation is exactly the contrary in the case of a request for the transfer of proceedings. Following the transfer, the executing Member State will be responsible for the further investigation, prosecution and judgment of the case. This entails a different kind of responsibility and requires room for a proper assessment when deciding on a request for the transfer of proceedings. This argument was largely shared and approved by participating experts and policy makers.

As a matter of fact, another characterising element of mutual recognition, the relativisation of the double criminality requirement (based on a list with offences where

45 For the sake of completeness, neither the Directive on the EIO nor the Council Framework Decision are examples of 'pure' mutual recognition: they present a system wherein grounds for refusal are applicable (EIO and EAW) of where execution is dependent on the availability of measures under domestic criminal procedure (EIO).

double criminality will not be checked; compare the Council Framework Decision on the EAW and the Directive on the EIO), would be inappropriate in the case of the transfer of criminal proceedings. It seems inconceivable that the receiving Member State prosecutes a suspect for something which is not punishable under its own domestic law.

When looking at the 2009 draft Council Framework Decision, we see that it has the structure of a mutual recognition instrument, yet not foreseeing mandatory execution. This is expressed amongst others by maintaining the term 'request'. Is this contradictory in a mutual recognition instrument? We are inclined to deny that.

As a matter of fact, the draft Council Framework Decision contains other elements that are convincing proof for its mutual recognition character. Most important is the fact that with a positive decision on a request for the transfer of proceedings, the executing Member State takes over the case and endorses in principle the decision to investigate and prosecute that has been taken by the authorities in the issuing Member State. Another element is the recognition of evidence that has been collected by the authorities of the issuing Member State during their investigations. One could also point to the limited number of grounds for refusal.

Our conclusion is that such an approach would strike the right balance. It can be expressed by defining the system of transfer of proceedings in criminal matters, set forth in a legal instrument, as follows:

> *The transfer of proceedings in criminal matters is a procedure in which a judicial authority of a Member State where proceedings have been opened ('issuing Member State'), issues a request to the judicial authority of another Member State ('receiving Member State') to take over these proceedings such in the interest of an efficient and proper administration of justice and taking into account the legitimate interests of suspects and victims.*

Other elements that stress the mutual recognition character may include the rule that after taking over a case from another Member State, the receiving Member State will treat the case with the same interest as any other similar domestic case. But this might be considered superfluous since, as a result of the decision to take over the case, it becomes a domestic case. We will propose a solution for the recognition of evidence in paragraph 5.7.

When this approach towards mutual recognition was presented during the second Working Conference, it gathered great support.

5.4 Criteria and conditions for issuing a request for the transfer of proceedings

We had many discussions about the criteria and the conditions for issuing a request for the transfer of proceedings during the interviews and the first Working Conference. It became clear that the criteria for issuing a request for the transfer of criminal proceedings are key when striving towards a well-functioning new legal instrument. Based on the outcome of our research, we developed the following ideas.

Criteria for (considering) the issuing of a request for transfer of proceedings

The fact that one of the criteria for considering a transfer of proceedings – mentioned in Article 7 of the draft Council Framework Decision and Article 8 of the 1972 Convention – is fulfilled does not mean that in all instances the other Member State is really in a better position to continue the investigation and prosecution of the case. Apart from stressing the underlying aim of promoting an efficient and proper administration of justice, which is still an important notion and requirement, an additional, supplementing criterion should be introduced: the other Member State is in a better position to prosecute. This will make clear that even when one of the criteria is applicable, and one could argue that a request for the transfer of proceedings is in the interest of an efficient and proper administration of justice (for example, because the interest of a victim would be better served), an important condition for the transfer of criminal proceedings – underlining or specifying the requirement of efficiency – should be that the judicial authority of the receiving Member State is overall in a better position to continue the proceedings.

> *The general criterion laid down in the phrase 'if that would improve the efficient and proper administration of justice' that precede the criteria to consider a transfer of criminal proceedings in Article 7 of the draft Council Framework Decision, should be supplemented by the condition that specifies the efficiency part as: the receiving Member State is in a better position to further investigate the criminal offence and prosecute the suspect.*

Conditions for the issuing of a request for the transfer of proceedings

It seems important to have a provision that describes which conditions must be met before issuing a request for the transfer of criminal proceedings. For example, the confirmation that all investigations in the issuing Member State that are a prerequisite for a successful prosecution of the case in the receiving Member State have been carried out. This can help prevent premature requests, not sufficiently motivated requests, and requests with only a very tenuous connection to the receiving Member State. The provision could be phrased as an obligation for the issuing authority to verify several conditions, similar to Article 6 of the Directive on the EIO.

As a part of this provision, an indication of the applicability of the criteria for the transfer of criminal proceedings may be required as well as – materialising the additional criterion proposed above – a motivation why in the opinion of the issuing authority, the judicial authority of the receiving Member State is in a better position to prosecute.

In this provision, we could also insert an obligation to ascertain that the rights of the suspect and the victim have been taken into account, as a materialisation of these requirements (explained in paragraph 5.5).

If the receiving authority is of the opinion that the conditions may not have been fulfilled by the issuing authority, further consultation and a request for additional information will be the appropriate solution.

Article X

1. *Before issuing a request for the transfer of proceedings, the issuing authority verifies that:*
   - *all necessary* investigations in the issuing Member State have been carried out*
   - *the rights of the suspect and the victim have been taken into account.*

2. *In its request for transfer of proceedings, the issuing authority pays special attention to:*
   - *indicating which of the criteria for the transfer of proceedings are applicable*
   - *motivating why the receiving authority would be in a better position to further prosecute the case.*

3. *Where the receiving authority has reason to believe that the conditions referred to in paragraphs 1 and 2 have not been met, it may consult the issuing authority and ask for additional information.*

** What is deemed necessary in this regard should be explained in a recital.*

A dedicated ground for refusal

The grounds for refusal laid down in Article 12 of the draft Council Framework Decision give little cause for discussion. They include agreed grounds for refusal, such as the absence of double criminality, bis in idem, immunity and the fact that prosecution is statute-barred.

Based on our research, an additional ground for refusal should be considered that mirrors the assessment that the issuing authority needs to make and enables the receiving judicial authority to filter out premature and ill-founded requests. The ground for refusal should apply if the receiving authority is of the opinion that a transfer of proceedings is not in the interest of an efficient and proper administration of justice. Such a ground for refusal would give the receiving authority a great deal of discretion. It would not only include the possibility for the receiving authority to assess whether it is indeed in a better position to prosecute, but also leave room for other arguments. The proposed ground for refusal would actually allow the receiving Member State to compare the prosecutorial action implied by the request for a transfer of proceedings with what it would do in a similar domestic case. This may include weighing different arguments concerning the priority of the case – its social impact – and the availability of human resources when the opportunity principle is applicable in the criminal procedure of the receiving Member State.

One could argue that this large degree of discretion would amount to legal uncertainty. However, it could be defended by pointing at the fact that it relates closely to the idea that the receiving authority will bear full responsibility for the prosecution of a case after it has agreed to take it over from the issuing Member State.

Further explanation of this ground for refusal as well as possibly some examples of how this ground for refusal should be used in practice could be subject of a recital.

> *Additional ground for refusal:*
> *-(x) if the request is not in the interest of an efficient and proper administration of justice.*

When drafting the provision on grounds for refusal, the EU legislator should not forget to insert an obligation to consult that is applicable in any case where the receiving authority considers invoking a ground for refusal – see further paragraph 5.7.

> *Before deciding to not accept/refuse the request, either in whole or in part, the receiving authority shall consult the issuing authority, by any appropriate means, and shall, where appropriate, request the issuing authority to supply any necessary information without delay.*

Conclusion

The conclusion from this paragraph is that a request for the transfer of criminal proceedings should be duly motivated and leave some discretion for the receiving Member State to decide whether to accept the transfer and to take over the case. Ultimately, a transfer of criminal proceedings must be based on a mutual agreement. Together the elements discussed in this paragraph amount to a handshake between the judicial authorities concerned.

5.5 Procedural rights

When discussing possible solutions for human rights issues which can arise in the context of a transfer of proceedings, it is important to bear in mind that the transfer is a form of judicial cooperation and thus primarily a procedure between the authorities of two Member States.

Therefore, it is difficult to determine where exactly the rights of the suspect come into play. From our point of view, a moderate or balanced approach might be preferable. It should be clear that the fundamental rights of the suspect must be considered, but we would not go so far as to state that this should amount to a right for the suspect to determine where he or she will be prosecuted. We also think that the legitimate interests of the suspect should be considered at the level of concrete standard setting, i.e., when contemplating the structure and wording of specific provisions of a dedicated regulation.

Based on this fundamental assumption and the knowledge gained in the preceding steps of our work, we formulated several concrete objectives that can be derived from the overarching goal of safeguarding the rights of the suspect as effectively as possible.

The possibility for the defence to ask for a transfer of proceedings

The first proposal that we discussed with the participants in the second Working Conference is that the suspect should have a possibility to demand a transfer of proceedings. As a solution, we proposed that a dedicated instrument should include a provision with the following content:

> *The issuing of a request for transfer of proceedings may be demanded by a suspect or accused person, or by a lawyer on his behalf, within the framework of applicable defense rights in conformity with national criminal procedure.*

It could be argued that there is no need for a formal request of the suspect since he or his defence lawyer could at any time approach the public prosecutor in charge with an informal request. However, a formal request has several advantages. It will need to be dealt with by the public prosecutor's office in a reasoned decision, which could be, when applicable under domestic law, liable for an appeal. This was seen as a clear advantage in terms of the suspect's rights.

Especially from a prosecutorial perspective, it was stressed that the impression must not be created that the suspect can choose where he wants to be charged. For the sake of clarity: in the concept of the transfer of proceedings between the judicial authorities of two states, there is no right for the suspect to decide where he prefers to be prosecuted.

Taking into account legitimate interests

The second objective that we discussed at the Working Conference was that the legitimate interests of the suspect should be taken into account by the acting authorities. A provision with the following wording could serve this purpose:

> *The transfer of proceedings in criminal matters is a judicial procedure in which a judicial authority of a Member State where proceedings have been opened ('issuing State'), issues a request to the judicial authority of another Member State ('receiving State') to take over these proceedings, such in the interest of an efficient and proper administration of justice and taking into account the legitimate interests of suspects and victims.*

This proposal met with broad approval among the participants of the second Working Conference, although it was noted that the wording remains on a rather abstract level and that the content of the duty constituted by it would have to be specified in individual cases.

The right for the suspect to be informed

Thirdly, we established that the suspect has a right to be informed about an intended transfer, to be assisted, and to give an opinion. The responsibility for ensuring these rights should in principle lie with the issuing authority. A phrase that could be suitable to promote this objective could be as follows:

> *The issuing authority shall inform, where appropriate, the person suspected of the offence of the intended transfer. The person suspected has the right to be assisted by a lawyer. If the suspected person presents an opinion on the transfer, this shall be taken into account.*

It could be added that:

> *When the suspect is already in the receiving Member State, he or she shall be informed via the authorities of that State.*

Participants supported the strengthening of the rights of the accused associated with this proposal, but also considered the relativisation ("where appropriate") to be necessary, because that would make it possible to take into account secrecy interests due to ongoing investigations.

Challenge of the decision to issue a request for a transfer of proceedings

We then proposed that the issuing authority should be obliged to inform the suspected person of its decision to pursue its request for a transfer and that the suspected person should be competent to use a legal remedy against this decision. As regards the latter, a possible solution could be worded as follows:

Member States shall ensure that the suspected person can use a legal remedy against this decision to transfer.

Alternatively, one could formulate as follows:

A suspected person may use a legal remedy against the decision to request a transfer, in accordance with the national law of the issuing Member State.

This proposal was controversially discussed in the second Working Conference. The prosecutors present were particularly sceptical and saw the danger that the proceedings would be unnecessarily complicated and drawn out by an appeal. It was also emphasised again that the impression must not be given that the suspect decides where he is prosecuted; this was seen as the very task of the public prosecutor's office. However, there were also voices that were more open to granting some form of legal protection to the suspect. If an appeal were to be provided, however, it would then also have to be clarified based on which criteria a decision on its merits would have to be made.

In addition, it should be noted that an adequate consideration of the rights of the suspect was often regarded as an essential prerequisite for a proposed regulation for the transfer of proceedings to gain the necessary broad acceptance in the legal policy debate. Some participants seemed to have the impression that, if one were to act only half-heartedly here and disregard the justified concerns of the suspect, this could jeopardise the success of the overall project in the long term. In order to avoid such undesirable developments, great care should therefore be taken in structuring the position of the accused.

The position of the victim

Finally, we put up for discussion the objectives that victims too should be informed of an intended transfer and that their view would need to be taken into account. A solution for this could be found in a paragraph with the following wording:

Before a request for transfer is made the transferring authority shall give due consideration to the interests of the victims of the offence and see to it that their rights under national law, and in accordance with Directive 2012/29/EU are fully respected. In particular, this includes, where possible, informing the victim of the intended transfer. The view of the victim shall be taken into account.

And:

In accordance with the national law of the issuing Member State, the victim may use a legal remedy against the decision to request a transfer of proceedings.

From discussions with respondents and participants in the Working Conferences, it was noted that especially in complex cases (e.g., a series of Internet fraud cases) the involvement of victims often encounters practical problems and, moreover, is often not even desired by the victims.

5.6 Jurisdiction

Jurisdiction is a subject where the results of our research are mitigated. We already mentioned that in paragraph 4.3.

The possible absence of jurisdiction did not come up as a primary concern during the interviews. We had the impression that a possible lack in jurisdiction is not perceived as a gap in the framework for the transfer of criminal proceedings. Indeed, Member States tend to have a broad basis for extraterritorial jurisdiction in their criminal law systems. Also, the theory of ubiquity is widely adhered to by Member States, extending their jurisdiction on the basis of the territoriality principle as the primary ground for jurisdiction.

We should be reminded of the fact that a provision on subsidiary jurisdiction turned out to be a breaking point in the negotiations on the draft Council Framework Decision in 2009.[46]

In our assessment, there are some gaps in the jurisdiction that Member States need to be able to successfully prosecute every offence that might be subject of a request for transfer of proceedings. A lacuna exists in the national law of a significant number of Member States in cases where an offence has been committed abroad by a person is a resident of a Member State but has not the nationality of that Member State (think of a Belgian living in Germany, who commits an offence while on holiday in Greece). This lacuna is caused by the reticent use of the so-called domicile principle as a ground for jurisdiction. The domicile principle mirrors the active nationality principle and extends a Member States' jurisdiction to persons with a habitual residence on the territory of that Member State but who do not have the Member States' nationality.[47]

In EU substantive criminal law, the domicile principle has been used as a ground to establish jurisdiction, but not consistently. Examples include the Council Framework Decision on combating terrorism (2002/475/JHA) and the Directive on combating terrorism (2017/541/EU)[48] which oblige Member States to establish jurisdiction over terrorist offences committed by one of their nationals 'or residents'. The Directive on

46 Doc. 16437/09 of November 2009, p. 3.
47 See A. Klip, *European Criminal Law*, Antwerp: Intersentia 2021, p. 263.
48 Article 19, par. 1, sub c.

preventing and combating trafficking in human beings and protecting its victims (2011/36/EU)[49] and the Directive on the fight against fraud to the Union's financial interests by means of criminal law ((EU) 2017/1371)[50] suggest the establishment of jurisdiction for habitual residents, but not in a mandatory way. Establishment of jurisdiction based on the domicile principle is again proposed in the Commission's proposal for a Directive on environmental crime (COM(2021)851).[51] One could argue that it is primarily a responsibility of the EU legislator to foresee jurisdiction for habitual residents and consequently prevent lacunas in jurisdiction in the case of an intended transfer of criminal proceedings. There are two strong reasons for the EU legislator to seriously consider this. From the perspective of developing an area of freedom, security and justice (Article 67 TFEU), it would make sense to consider introducing the domicile principle as a general ground for jurisdiction, given the principle of non-discrimination of EU citizens independently where they choose to reside that is at stake. Secondly, it would help build a comprehensive framework for judicial cooperation when this remaining gap in jurisdiction is solved. It would help prevent possible impunity and provide an alternative to the application of the EAW where this is deemed too intrusive.

Another relevant aspect is that of the possible establishment of subsidiary or complementary jurisdiction, tied to the transfer of criminal proceedings. The 1972 Convention (Article 2) and the draft Council Framework Decision (Article 5) propose such a form of subsidiary jurisdiction, in what we could describe as a two-step approach. The idea is that States first establish jurisdiction to be able to prosecute any offence to which the law of another Member State is applicable. A request for transfer of proceedings then can subsequently activate this jurisdiction in an individual case.[52] This two-step approach continues to be criticised by some. After analysis, we feel that the approach could be simplified. In a way, it seems exaggerated to oblige Member States to establish virtual jurisdiction for every offence committed in another Member State. And when taken literally, it is quite understandable that for some Member States this may be controversial. Why not leave the first step out? One could argue that it suffices to oblige Member States to establish complementary jurisdiction for offences that are subject of a transfer of proceedings, in case acting as a receiving Member State, their own rules on jurisdiction would fall short.

A variation of this solution would be to simply create a basis for complementary jurisdiction in the legal instrument,[53] that Member States may choose to implement in their legislation – a facultative ground for jurisdiction.

49 Article 10, par. 2, sub c.
50 Article 11, par. 3, sub a.
51 Article 12, par. 1, sub d.
52 See Explanatory Report to the European Convention on the Transfer of Proceedings in Criminal Matters, p. 14.
53 Or: given by the instrument and to implemented in national law.

> *The executing Member State may use jurisdiction from the issuing Member State based on the request when the executing Member State has no jurisdiction to prosecute the case and the suspect is a habitual resident of the receiving Member State.*

Another solution to cover possible lacuna in jurisdiction could be found in the need to find a solution for some specific situations that occur in daily practice of judicial cooperation in the EU. This would be more of a pragmatic approach, with a limited effect, to be considered when an agreement on a general rule as proposed above turns out to be impossible. Two situations may serve as a ground for the establishment of complementary jurisdiction in this regard.

Firstly, one could think of the situation where an EAW is refused by the executing Member State or otherwise cannot be materialised (for example, because of a temporary suspension of the decision to surrender a person due to the poor detention conditions in the issuing Member State).[54]

> *When a request for a transfer of proceedings follows a situation wherein an EAW is refused by the executing Member State or otherwise cannot be materialised, the jurisdiction of the executing Member State may – based on a request for the transfer of proceedings – extend to the facts committed in the issuing Member State as mentioned in the request when the executing Member State would otherwise lack jurisdiction to prosecute.*

A second situation may also inspire the inclusion of a ground for complementary jurisdiction in a new legal instrument for the transfer of proceedings. When it is felt desirable that prosecution of a number of suspects accused of organized crime is concentrated in one particular Member State, it is advisable that the suspects can be equally prosecuted for every other offence they are accused of, in the proceedings in that Member State. This was discussed during our research project as part of the challenges that may occur in Category I cases. It should be noted that this argument for considering the establishment of complementary jurisdiction was also put forward, when alternatives for a rule on jurisdiction were being looked after, during the negotiations on the draft Council Framework Decision in 2009.[55]

> *When proceedings are pending in the executing Member State that imply the same suspect or the same facts as mentioned in a request for transfer of proceedings, the jurisdiction of the executing Member State may – based on a request for the transfer of proceedings – extend to the facts committed in the issuing Member State as mentioned in the request when the executing Member State would otherwise lack jurisdiction to prosecute.*

---

54 Court of Justice of the EU, 5 April 2016, C-404/15 and C-659/15 PPU (Aranyosi & Căldăraru).

55 Doc. 16437/09 of November 2009, p. 5-7.

5.7 Procedure, communication, translation and costs

The added value of (direct) consultation between the issuing and receiving authorities

Experts agree that a good communication is *the* best practice in judicial cooperation. It is therefore logical and advisable to point to consultation at every instance in the procedure for the transfer of proceedings where additional explanation or better understanding of each other's position may be needed to bring the process forward. In fact, it is wise to prescribe a step-by-step procedure to be followed to successfully perform a transfer of criminal proceedings, stressing the possibility of consultation every time where it may have added value.

This starts with prior consultation about an intended request for the transfer of proceedings. Respondents in our research project are regretting the little use of prior consultation. In their view, prior consultation may help prevent premature and ill-founded requests. In fact, prior consultation may offer the best opportunity to start exchanging views about which Member State is in the best position to further investigate and prosecute a case. It can also help discuss what is the best instrument to effectuate the transfer – including the possibility of a spontaneous exchange of information, which will remain to be an alternative to a formal transfer of proceedings in some situations. Furthermore, prior consultation can be used to address practical issues, like which supporting information the receiving authority would need to be able to decide swiftly on the request. However, the general opinion is that prior consultation should not be mandatory. It is superfluous in clear cut cases.

In the context of prior consultation, the issuing authority may question the receiving authority on what to expect after a possible transfer of proceedings. This may include, amongst other things, the modality of prosecution that will be used in the receiving Member State, the expected timeframe and if possible, the expected sanction. This in a sense provides the issuing authority with 'the whole picture'.

After a request for a transfer of proceedings has been issued, consultation is advised at every stage of the procedure for the transfer of criminal proceedings, notably:
- when the conditions for the issuing of a request do not seem to have been met or when the request is not sufficiently motivated in this respect
- before invoking a possible ground for refusal
- in the case of extraordinary costs
- when having taken over the case, the receiving authority decides to drop the charges.

In paragraphs 5.3, 5.6 and hereafter in this paragraph respectively, drafting proposals are suggested for provisions that encourage the use of consultation.

Standard forms

Based on our research, the introduction of standardised forms to perform and process a transfer of proceedings could improve the current practice considerably. We would think of three different standard forms:

- Form A: a standard form for the request for a transfer of proceedings
- Form B: a standard form for confirmation of the receipt of a request[56]
- Form C: a standard form for feedback on the outcome of proceedings to the issuing authority after the proceedings have been completed in the executing Member State

A standard form for the request for a transfer of proceedings

Almost all respondents in our research project agreed that a uniform, easy to perform procedure for the request of a transfer of proceedings presumes the use of a standard form. A frequently heard concern is that such a form should not be too long and complicated.[57] How to strike the right balance between providing the information needed by the receiving authority without being too elaborate and complicate things? What should the form include?

Based on our research and the discussion on this subject in workshops in the first and the second Working Conferences, the following parts of information should be included in the standard form that is a solid basis for a request for the transfer of proceedings:

- Information on the issuing authority (name, contact details, etc.)
- A description of the facts, a resumé of the investigations, a summary of the evidence
- A legal qualification of the facts
- Information about the statute of limitations
- Personal details of the suspect (name, d.o.b., etc.)
- Personal details of the victim(s)
- A statement that the conditions for issuing a transfer have been fulfilled (see paragraph 5.4)

Translation

We have addressed on several occasions in this report the challenge posed by the need for translation in practice. It can already discourage judicial authorities from issuing a request for the transfer of proceedings. In any event, translation will be necessary. We considered, together with our respondents, ways to reduce the need

---

56 Compare the form in Annex B to the Directive on the EIO.

57 See the annex to the 2009 draft Council Framework Decision.

for translation, for example by limiting the parts of the case file that should be translated. However, this will not work in practice. Judges, defendants and their lawyers will always want access to all information in a case file, and they are entitled to require that. The incumbent costs of translation are a challenge on their own – subject to a proposal below.

Nevertheless, a future legal instrument can set out some clear rules about translation. It seems logical to distinguish between the translation needed for the request (form A and supporting documents) and the translation of the case file after the acceptance of a request for transfer of proceedings.

In the first phase, the initiative for a transfer of proceedings is taken by the issuing authority.[58] As a demanding party, it will be appropriate to take care of the request including its translation into the language of the receiving Member State or another language that the receiving Member State has indicated to accept.

For several reasons, it is advisable that the receiving or executing authority takes care of the translation needed to further prosecute the case in its Member State after acceptance of the request to transfer. The authorities in the executing Member State are in the best position to assess what will be needed in respect of translation of the case file with regard to the court proceedings: which parts of the file should be translated, whether a certified translation is required, etc. It will also be easier to get a reliable and high-quality translation into its own language in the Member State concerned.

> *The standard form A for the request and its supporting documents shou/d be trans/ated by the issuing authority into the Janguage of the receiving Member State or in another Janguage indicated by the receiving State.*
>
> *After lhe decision to accept the transfer of proceedings, the executing authority is responsib/e for trans/ating al/ other parts of the case file.*

Costs

Closely related to the topic of translation is the issue of costs. Costs related to the transfer of criminal proceedings are primarily the costs for translation of the request and the case file. The question who is to pay the costs of the transfer of criminal proceedings can consequently be answered in parallel with the answer to the question which Member State should take care of which part of the translation: the issuing authority bears the costs for the request and anything else needed before the actual

58 Respondents in our research project also urged to make it possible for the requested Member State to initiate a procedure for the transfer of proceedings (asking the issuing Member State to consider transferring the proceedings that is conducting).

transmission of the case after acceptance of the request by the receiving Member State. This can be expressed by a formula that leans on the fact that this division coincides with the territory (of the issuing Member State and the receiving/executing Member State) where these costs will arise.

In the case of the acceptance of a request for the transfer of proceedings, the receiving Member State takes over the case and will proceed with its investigation, prosecution, court proceedings and finally the execution of a possible sentence. This all involves incurring costs. One could argue that these costs stem from the request by the issuing authority, and it may therefore be logical to make the issuing authority (at least in part) responsible for all incumbent costs. However, the view is broadly shared that this is an avenue that we should pursue. Part of the acceptance of the case by the receiving authority is its willingness to cover the costs for further prosecution of the case. It is widely accepted that this is a fair solution because Member States will sometimes act as an issuing Member State and sometimes as a receiving Member State.

The support for this solution could weaken when there is a big gap between the number of requests that a Member State receives and issues, a situation that might occur as explained in paragraph 3.2. This makes it wise to insert an exception to the basic cost regime, as foreseen in Article 21 of the Directive on the EIO in the case of costs for the execution that may be deemed exceptionally high – by the number of cases that a particular issuing Member State wants the receiving Member State to take over. Likewise, the exception may be useful when a request is made to transfer a very big and complex criminal case of organized or financial crime. In both instances, the exception should consist of further consultation between the authorities of the Member States involved with the aim of finding a solution by changing the request or sharing (some of) the costs related to the further prosecution of the case.[59]

> *Costs (for the execution of the request) sho/1 be borne by the Member Stote of the receiving outhority, except for costs orising exclusive/y in the terri tory of the issuing Member Stote.*
>
> *Where the receiving authority considers that the costs for the execution of the request may be deemed exceptionally high, it may consult with the issuing authority on whether and how the costs could be shared, or the request could be modified.*

59 An interesting, yet exceptional example, is provided by a case in which a Dutch Court ordered that the Netherlands should pay compensation to an acquitted person for the time he had spent in pre-trial detention in the issuing Member State before the transfer of proceedings to the Netherlands (Court of Appeal Amsterdam 22 December 2020, no. 13/457743-08 (not published).

Timeframes for a receipt of the request and for deciding on a request for transfer of proceedings

A lack of clarity about when to expect a decision on a request for the transfer of proceedings and even silence on the receipt of the request are annoyances that are often experienced by judicial authorities in the current practice of the transfer of proceedings.

This situation could simply be resolved by introducing timeframes in the future legal instrument for the transfer of criminal proceedings in the EU. One could think of a timeframe for confirming the receipt of a request (by sending standard form B to the issuing authority). This confirmation should follow as soon as possible, and at the latest within two weeks of the receipt of the request. The two-week time delay allows for an internal transmission of the request to the competent authority in case this is another authority than the one that initially received the request.

Even more important is providing a timeframe for the decision on the request for the transfer of proceedings. After discussing what would be an appropriate timeframe during interviews and in the Working Conferences, it seems that 60 days is reasonable. This delay enables the authorities of the receiving Member State to check all relevant elements for their decision on the request for the transfer of proceedings and have all internal and external (with the issuing authority) consultations that might be necessary to this effect. Only in exceptional circumstances, and after consulting the issuing authority, is an extension of this delay with another 30 days conceivable.

> *The receiving authority confirms the receipt of the request for a transfer of proceedings by sending standard form B to the issuing authority, as soon as possible and no later than 30 days after the receipt.*
>
> *The receiving authority takes a decision on the request for transfer of proceedings within 60 days after the receipt of the request. If it is not possible to respect this time limit, this time limit may – after consulting the issuing authority – be extended with a maximum of 30 days.*

5.8 After the decision to take over the proceedings: further execution

The issue of regulating the situation after a positive decision to take over proceedings is closely related to the outcome of the discussion on mutual recognition (paragraph 5.3).

In fact, the overriding argument to ensure a great deal of discretion for the receiving authority to decide whether or not to accept a request for the transfer of proceedings is the full responsibility of the receiving Member State for all further proceedings.

The latter should be expressed in the main rule that the further investigation, prosecution, judgment of the case as well as the execution of possible sentences is based on the law of the executing Member State.

> *After the decision by the receiving authority to take over the proceedings/accept the transfer of proceedings, further proceedings are governed by the law of the executing (receiving) Member State.*

A second aspect is closely related. Although it bears responsibility and enjoys discretion for the further proceedings, the receiving Member State builds on the content of the criminal proceedings as it was at the moment of accepting the request for transfer and taking over the case. Further investigation and prosecution can only be successful when the results of the proceedings in the issuing Member State can be used and built upon. This is an element of mutual recognition and expresses the mutual trust that is necessary as a basis for successfully performing a transfer of proceedings.

Once transferred, after the decision by the receiving authority to take over proceedings, further proceedings should – as a general approach – be governed by the law of the executing Member State. That not only applies to the applicability of procedural law, but also to the substantive criminal law. General approach in this context means: except for some specific topics and discussions on evidence and sanctioning that will be dealt with below. The approach is so obvious that participants in the second Working Conference expressed some doubt as to whether it needs explicit regulation.

In this respect, accepting this general approach not only strengthens the mutual trust as underlying principle of the cooperation in criminal matters between Member States of the EU but also the flexibility required for an effective and practical instrument for the transfer of proceedings.

It is advisable that any difficulties, for example when collected evidence is considered to be contrary to fundamental principles of the law of the receiving Member State, could best be anticipated and discussed in the framework of prior consultation, as explained in paragraph 5.7.

Evidence and sanctions

In the discussion to what extent exceptions on the general approach on the applicability of the law of the executing Member State are (absolutely) necessary, two topics required special attention: evidence and sanctions.

Aspects of evidence form a delicate issue in many respects. There are fundamental differences between the systems of the law on criminal evidence between the Member States. The admissibility of evidence and its use in criminal proceedings in the receiving Member State may – despite transfer of proceedings – depend on the way in which evidence was gathered in the issuing Member State. (Even) after the transfer of proceedings, the authorities in the receiving Member State might still depend on further activities and actions from authorities in the issuing Member State, such as the possibility to have police officers act as a witness in court proceedings in the executing Member State or by video conference, partly as part of the important fair trial right for the accused to have – at least at some point during the criminal charge – witnesses against him questioned, a right that was recently articulated by the Keskin decision of the ECrtHR.[60]

There are several (alternative) options to overcome or avoid problems and obstacles here. Emphasising a certain preference for prosecution in the Member State where the majority of the evidence is gathered is one of them. In some cases, an EIO or laying down provisions in a JIT contract can help. But there is no clear or general approach within the EU defining a rule on admissibility of evidence so far. A rule that warrants the use of evidence that might not be allowed in domestic procedures could be a step to far. On the other hand: a discussed general provision that confirms the value of the evidence gathered in the issuing Member State was not found necessary.

For that reason, there is a need for the explanation of two fundamental principles as minimum provision and minimum guarantee at the outside of the regulation of the transfer of proceedings, more or less a 'first step' addition to Article 17 of the 2009 Draft Council Framework Decision.

The first principle is that evidence transferred by the issuing authority shall not be denied admission in proceedings in the executing Member State on the mere ground that the evidence was gathered in another Member State. Evidence legally obtained abroad can be allowed and be admissible in domestic proceedings. The character of a minimum provision ('mere ground') on the other hand stresses the fact that (and leaves the need for) flexibility for Member States to uphold certain specific conditions and demands for the admissibility and use of (certain types of) evidence gathered abroad, such as the (non) use of *de auditu* statements (hearsay evidence), connected to the responsibility for a fair trial and the need to avoid miscarriages of justice. It is obviously up to the court to assess the evidence.

In this respect, an explicit provision seems desirable according to which the receiving Member State cannot be expected to accept (make admissible or use) evidence that as such or – given the procedures to collect the evidence in the issuing State – is contrary to the very fundamental principles of law of this executing Member State, despite the risk that discussions may evolve as to whether certain characteristics of

60 ECrtHR 19 January 2021, appl.no. 2205/16 (Keskin v. the Netherlands).

domestic law are to be seen as 'fundamental principles of law'. The necessity of this exception lies in its very nature.

> *Evidence transferred by the issuing authority shall not be denied admission in proceedings in the executing Member State on the mere ground that the evidence was gathered in another Member State.*
>
> *The evidence collected in the issuing Member State may be used in proceedings in the executing Member State, provided that the evidence or procedures used to collect the evidence are not contrary to the fundamental principles of law of the executing Member State.*

Where the issue of the applicable sanctions is concerned, it can be argued that the transfer of proceedings should not place the accused in a worse situation – as far as the threatened penalty is concerned – than without the transfer. That would lead to the *lex mitior* principle that the maximum sentence to be imposed should be the lowest of the two Member States involved or be the maximum sanction possible in the issuing Member State.

Nevertheless, there is reason to follow the general approach, leading to the conclusion that in the Member State of the receiving authority, the sanction applicable to the offence shall be described by its own law unless that law provides otherwise. Even when the offence has been perpetrated (exclusively) in the territory of the issuing Member State or when proceedings in the executing Member State are based on subsidiary jurisdiction.[61]

Most systems allow the sentencing judge to take aspects of the sanction regime in the issuing Member State into account.[62] This could be an appropriate way to deal with the difference between the maximum penalties in the issuing and executing Member States. This is especially the case where there are reasons to accord some extra weight to the applicable penalty in the issuing Member State, most prominently when the offence has been committed (exclusively) on the territory of the issuing Member States. Such a solution can strike the right balance.

> *The executing authority may take into consideration, in accordance with its national law, the (maximum) penalty foreseen in the law of the issuing Member State, when the offence has been perpetrated (exclusively) in the territory of the issuing Member State.*

61 There is no need for the exception that Article 17, par. 6, of the 2009 Draft Framework Decision provides in this regard.

62 It should be noted that it will be very difficult to value differences between Member States without broad knowledge of aspects of the system of execution of sanctions in theory and practice, such as the possibilities for and practice of early (conditional) release, pardon, etc.

The need for suspension; the possibility of reopening

It was put forward in the on-site interviews and in the discussions during the Working Conferences that, for practical and theoretical reasons, it should be avoided that proceedings and investigations continue in the issuing Member State after the taking over of procedure by the receiving Member State. On the other hand, the issuing Member State does not and should not lose competence or at least not lose it definitely; this could lead to impunity.

That leads to the arguable need for a provision at EU level for the discontinuation (suspension, temporary abandonment) of the case after the acceptance of the transfer of proceedings in the issuing Member State.[63]

This discontinuation is connected to the expectation of the outcome of further proceedings in the receiving Member State. That expectation calls, first of all, for a proper rule according to which the receiving Member State will, in all cases, inform the issuing Member State within due time or within a certain, fixed period of time, about the outcome of the proceedings. Preferably by using a standard form (the proposed standard form C).

When the case has reached a final decision by a court, the ne bis in idem rule applies and will limit the possibilities for any further action by the issuing Member State. The situation is different when the issuing Member State is informed that the outcome of proceedings after transfer has been the decision to drop the case. There is then the possibility for the issuing Member State to consider opening or reopening the case in a way that does not contravene the ne bis in idem principle. Considering the case and or – at least – deciding not to (re)open the case might be necessary in Member States which have the legality principle. These Member States therefore have a legitimate interest to be adequately informed about the outcome of the case by the executing Member State.

There is no fundamental difference between Member States with the opportunity principle respectively with the legality principle. In both systems, (re)opening the case is possible. To a certain extent, the legal situation is comparable or similar to that in which the transfer request is withdrawn or the case is re-transferred to the issuing Member State. Therefore, there is no need to make a distinction between Member States in the general approach that the issuing Member State may open or reopen proceedings if the executing Member State informs it of its decision to discontinue the proceedings related to the facts underlying the request. The rules on

63 The provision laid down in Article 16, par. 1, of the 2009 Draft Framework Decision ("except for any necessary investigations, including judicial assistance to the receiving authority") seems unnecessary where further judicial cooperation (such as executing an EIO) does not require that national proceedings remain open.)

evidence as discussed above may apply similarly. To promote flexibility, the matter of regulation of the (further) consequences of a (re)opening of the case can be left to the national law of the Member States, provided that at EU level the duty to (properly) inform the issuing Member State is guaranteed.

> *After the decision of the receiving authority to take over the proceedings/accept the transfer of proceedings, the proceedings related to the facts underlying the request for transfer shall, in accordance with national law, be discontinued or suspended in the issuing Member State.*
>
> *The issuing Member State may open or reopen proceedings when the executing Member State informs it of its decision to discontinue the proceedings related to the facts underlying the request.*

6 The aim: a comprehensive framework for judicial cooperation in the EU

A well-functioning system of judicial cooperation is vitally important for criminal justice in the EU. This applies both to the effectiveness of law enforcement and combatting all forms of crime, as well as for an adequate protection of the fundamental rights of the persons involved.

Our research project aims to contribute to such a well-functioning system of judicial cooperation by formulating proposals to improve the transfer of proceedings as one of the basic tools for cooperation. With some improvements and based on a new set of clear legal rules, the transfer of proceedings may play a greater role within the framework of judicial cooperation between Member States and expand its scope and effectiveness.

Two decades of legislative activity have resulted in a set of EU instruments for judicial cooperation. This acquis must be maintained, improved and expanded. Judicial cooperation should keep pace with globalisation, trends in criminal activity and with the digitalisation of society. It should also embrace technological innovation (see paragraph 2.4).

This research project proves that it is important to continue studying and evaluating the functioning of the system of judicial cooperation in everyday practice. This increases the knowledge and the *know-how* of judicial authorities. There are currently several mechanisms for evaluation in place. The European Commission conducts an evaluation of the implementation of new instruments after their adoption and continues to do so afterwards.[64] This evaluation can lead to the initiation of an infringement procedure against Member States which do not comply with their duty to implement the EU legislation properly. We know that this sanctioning mechanism is necessary. But it may have a chilling effect: Member States and experts could be reluctant to share the challenges that they experience in practice.

---

64 For example, Report from the European Commission on the implementation of Directive 2014/41/EU regarding the European Investigation Order in criminal matters, COM(2021) 409 final.

Another mechanism is the cycle of mutual evaluations of judicial cooperation in the EU set up by the Council. These thematic evaluations allow a more profound vision on the practical use of judicial cooperation instruments, based on on-site visits and interviews conducted by peers.[65] We can also point to the extensive casework of Eurojust. Perhaps most accurate and promising are the analyses of the European Judicial Network. The EJN might be the ideal forum for a transparent discussion on practical experiences with the judicial cooperation framework, by well-informed experts. In our opinion, academia could also do more: scholars should contribute their analysis, by conducting targeted research into the practice. This is in line with our research philosophy, explained in paragraph 1.4.

Currently, apart from ideas to improve the application of instruments such as the EAW and the EIO, the need for new, additional legislation is felt on the subject of electronic evidence (proposals for legislation – a regulation and a directive – are being discussed in the European Parliament),[66] the transfer of proceedings, and – in our opinion – the cross-border use of videoconferencing for trial purposes.

Together with a well-functioning instrument on the transfer of proceedings, a dedicated instrument on the use of videoconferencing to let a suspect who is residing in another Member State stand trial by videoconference may complete the toolbox for judicial cooperation in the EU with two instruments that can be a useful addition and alternative to the use of the EAW, and reactivate instruments that have so far been little used in practice – the Council Framework Decision on the application of the principle of mutual recognition to decisions on supervision measures as an alternative to provisional detention (2008/829/JHA) and the Council Framework Decision on the application of the principle of mutual recognition to judgments and probation decisions with a view to the supervision of probation measures and alternative sanctions (2008/947/JHA).

As a final step towards a comprehensive framework for the judicial cooperation, clear guidelines should be developed on which instrument should be used in which situation, and how it should be used.

65 The 9th round of mutual evaluations is currently taking place, the topic being the mutual recognition legal instruments in the field of deprivation or restriction of liberty.

66 Proposal for a Regulation of the European Parliament and of the Council on European Production and Preservation Orders for electronic evidence in criminal matters, COM(2018) 225 final.

Annex 1 European Convention on the Transfer of Proceedings in Criminal Matters

COUNCIL OF EUROPE

CONSEIL DE L'EUROPE

European Treaty Series – No. 73

European Convention on the Transfer of Proceedings in Criminal Matters

Strasbourg, 15.V.1972

The member States of the Council of Europe, signatory hereto,

Considering that the aim of the Council of Europe is the achievement of greater unity between its Members;

Desiring to supplement the work which they have already accomplished in the field of criminal law with a view to arriving at more just and efficient sanctions;

Considering it useful to this end to ensure, in a spirit of mutual confidence, the organisation of criminal proceedings on the international level, in particular, by avoiding the disadvantages resulting from conflicts of competence,

Have agreed as follows:

PART I. Definitions

Article 1

For the purposes of this Convention
(a) "offence" comprises acts dealt with under the criminal law and those dealt with under the legal provisions listed in Appendix III to this Convention on condition

that where an administrative authority is competent to deal with the offence it must be possible for the person concerned to have the case tried by a court;

(b) "sanction" means any punishment or other measure incurred or pronounced in respect of an offence or in respect of a violation of the legal provisions listed in Appendix III.

PART II. Competence

Article 2

1. For the purposes of applying this Convention, any Contracting State shall have competence to prosecute under its own criminal law any offence to which the law of another Contracting State is applicable.
2. The competence conferred on a Contracting State exclusively by virtue of paragraph 1 of this Article may be exercised only pursuant to a request for proceedings presented by another Contracting State.

Article 3

Any Contracting State having competence under its own law to prosecute an offence may, for the purposes of applying this Convention, waive or desist from proceedings against a suspected person who is being or will be prosecuted for the same offence by another Contracting State. Having regard to Article 21, paragraph 2, any such decision to waive or to desist from proceedings shall be provisional pending a final decision in the other Contracting State.

Article 4

The requested State shall discontinue proceedings exclusively grounded on Article 2 when to its knowledge the right of punishment is extinguished under the law of the requesting State for a reason other than time-limitation, to which Articles 10 *(c)*, 11 *(f)* and *(g)*, 22, 23 and 26 in particular apply.

Article 5

The provisions of Part III of this Convention do not limit the competence given to a requested State by its municipal law in regard to prosecutions.

PART III. Transfer of Proceedings

SECTION 1. REQUEST FOR PROCEEDINGS

Article 6

1. When a person is suspected of having committed an offence under the law of a Contracting State, that State may request another Contracting State to take proceedings in the cases and under the conditions provided for in this Convention.

2. If under the provisions of this Convention a Contracting State may request another Contracting State to take proceedings, the competent authorities of the first State shall take that possibility into consideration.

Article 7

1. Proceedings may not be taken in the requested State unless the offence in respect of which the proceedings are requested would be an offence if committed in its territory and when, under these circumstances, the offender would be liable to sanction under its own law also.
2. If the offence was committed by a person of public status or against a person, an institution or any thing of public status in the requesting State, it shall be considered in the requested State as having been committed by a person of public status or against such a person, an institution or any thing corresponding, in the latter State, to that against which it was actually committed.

Article 8

1. A Contracting State may request another Contracting State to take proceedings in any one or more of the following cases:
   (a) if the suspected person is ordinarily resident in the requested State;
   (b) if the suspected person is a national of the requested State or if that State is his State of origin;
   (c) if the suspected person is undergoing or is to undergo a sentence involving deprivation of liberty in the requested State;
   (d) if proceedings for the same or other offences are being taken against the suspected person in the requested State;
   (e) if it considers that transfer of the proceedings is warranted in the interests of arriving at the truth and in particular that the most important items of evidence are located in the requested State;
   (f) if it considers that the enforcement in the requested State of a sentence if one were passed is likely to improve the prospects for the social rehabilitation of the person sentenced;
   (g) if it considers that the presence of the suspected person cannot be ensured at the hearing of proceedings in the requesting State and that his presence in person at the hearing of proceedings in the requested State can be ensured;
   (h) if it considers that it could not itself enforce a sentence if one were passed, even by having recourse to extradition, and that the requested State could do so.
2. Where the suspected person has been finally sentenced in a Contracting State, that State may request the transfer of proceedings in one or more of the cases referred to in paragraph 1 of this Article only if it cannot itself enforce the sentence, even by having recourse to extradition, and if the other Contracting State does not accept enforcement of a foreign judgment as a matter of principle or refuses to enforce such sentence.

Article 9

1. The competent authorities in the requested State shall examine the request for proceedings made in pursuance of the preceding Articles. They shall decide, in accordance with their own law, what action to take thereon.
2. Where the law of the requested State provides for the punishment of the offence by an administrative authority, that State shall, as soon as possible, so inform the requesting State unless the requested State has made a declaration under paragraph 3 of this Article.
3. Any Contracting State may at the time of signature, or when depositing its instrument of ratification, acceptance or accession, or at any later date indicate, by declaration addressed to the Secretary General of the Council of Europe, the conditions under which its domestic law permits the punishment of certain offences by an administrative authority. Such a declaration shall replace the notification envisaged in paragraph 2 of this Article.

Article 10

The requested State shall not take action on the request:
(a) if the request does not comply with the provisions of Articles 6, paragraph 1, and 7, paragraph 1;
(b) if the institution of proceedings is contrary to the provisions of Article 35;
(c) if, at the date on the request, the time-limit for criminal proceedings has already expired in the requesting State under the legislation of that State.

Article 11

Save as provided for in Article 10 the requested State may not refuse acceptance of the request in whole or in part, except in any one or more of the following cases:
(a) if it considers that the grounds on which the request is based under Article 8 are not justified;
(b) if the suspected person is not ordinarily resident in the requested State;
(c) if the suspected person is not a national of the requested State and was not ordinarily resident in the territory of that State at the time of the offence;
(d) if it considers that the offence for which proceedings are requested is an offence of a political nature or a purely military or fiscal one;
(e) if it considers that there are substantial grounds for believing that the request for proceedings was motivated by considerations of race, religion, nationality or political opinion;
(f) if its own law is already applicable to the offence and if at the time of the receipt of the request proceedings were precluded by lapse of time according to that law; Article 26, paragraph 2, shall not apply in such a case;
(g) if its competence is exclusively grounded on Article 2 and if at the time of the receipt of the request proceedings would be precluded by lapse of time according to its law, the prolongation of the timelimit by six months under the terms of Article 23 being taken into consideration;
(h) if the offence was committed outside the territory of the requesting State;

(i) if proceedings would be contrary to the international undertakings of the requested State;
(j) if proceedings would be contrary to the fundamental principles of the legal system of the requested State;
(k) if the requesting State has violated a rule of procedure laid down in this Convention.

Article 12

1. The requested State shall withdraw its acceptance of the request if, subsequent to this acceptance, a ground mentioned in Article 10 of this Convention for not taking action on the request becomes apparent.
2. The requested State may withdraw its acceptance of the request:
   (a) if it becomes apparent that the presence in person of the suspected person cannot be ensured at the hearing of proceedings in that State or that any sentence, which might be passed, could not be enforced in that State;
   (b) if one of the grounds for refusal mentioned in Article 11 becomes apparent before the case is brought before a court; or
   (c) in other cases, if the requesting State agrees.

SECTION 2. TRANSFER PROCEDURE

Article 13

1. All requests specified in this Convention shall be made in writing. They, and all communications necessary for the application of this Convention, shall be sent either by the Ministry of Justice of the requesting State to the Ministry of Justice of the requested State or, by virtue of special mutual arrangement, direct by the authorities of the requesting State to those of the requested State; they shall be returned by the same channel.
2. In urgent cases, requests and communications may be sent through the International Criminal Police Organisation (INTERPOL).
3. Any Contracting State may, by declaration addressed to the Secretary General of the Council of Europe, give notice of its intention to adopt insofar as it itself is concerned rules of transmission other than those laid down in paragraph 1 of this Article.

Article 14

If a Contracting State considers that the information supplied by another Contracting State is not adequate to enable it to apply this Convention, it shall ask for the necessary additional information. It may prescribe a date for the receipt of such information.

Article 15

1. A request for proceedings shall be accompanied by the original, or a certified copy, of the criminal file and all other necessary documents. However, if the

suspected person is remanded in custody in accordance with the provisions of Section 5 and if the requesting State is unable to transmit these documents at the same time as the request for proceedings, the documents may be sent subsequently.

2. The requesting State shall also inform the requested State in writing of any procedural acts performed or measures taken in the requesting State after the transmission of the request which have a bearing on the proceedings. This communication shall be accompanied by any relevant documents.

Article 16

1. The requested State shall promptly communicate its decision on the request for proceedings to the requesting State.
2. The requested State shall also inform the requesting State of a waiver of proceedings or of the decision taken as a result of proceedings. A certified copy of any written decision shall be transmitted to the requesting State.

Article 17

If the competence of the requested State is exclusively grounded on Article 2 that State shall inform the suspected person of the request for proceedings with a view to allowing him to present his views on the matter before that State has taken a decision on the request.

Article 18

1. Subject to paragraph 2 of this Article, no translation of the documents relating to the application of this Convention shall be required.
2. Any Contracting State may, at the time of signature or when depositing its instrument of ratification, acceptance or accession, by declaration addressed to the Secretary General of the Council of Europe, reserve the right to require that, with the exception of the copy of the written decision referred to in Article 16, paragraph 2, the said documents be accompanied by a translation. The other Contracting States shall send the translations in either the national language of the receiving State or such one of the official languages of the Council of Europe as the receiving State shall indicate. However, such an indication is not obligatory. The other Contracting States may claim reciprocity.
3. This Article shall be without prejudice to any provisions concerning translation of requests and supporting documents that may be contained in agreements or arrangements now in force or that may be concluded between two or more Contracting States.

Article 19

Documents transmitted in application of this Convention need not be authenticated.

Article 20

Contracting Parties shall not claim from each other the refund of any expenses resulting from the application of this Convention.

SECTION 3. EFFECTS IN THE REQUESTING STATE OF A REQUEST FOR PROCEEDINGS

Article 21

1. When the requesting State has requested proceedings, it can no longer prosecute the suspected person for the offence in respect of which the proceedings have been requested or enforce a judgment which has been pronounced previously in that State against him for that offence. Until the requested State's decision on the request for proceedings has been received, the requesting State shall, however, retain its right to take all steps in respect of prosecution, short of bringing the case to trial, or, as the case may be, allowing the competent administrative authority to decide on the case.
2. The right of prosecution and of enforcement shall revert to the requesting State:
   (a) if the requested State informs it of a decision in accordance with Article 10 not to take action on the request;
   (b) if the requested State informs it of a decision in accordance with Article 11 to refuse acceptance of the request;
   (c) if the requested State informs it of a decision in accordance with Article 12 to withdraw acceptance of the request;
   (d) if the requested State informs it of a decision not to institute proceedings or discontinue them;
   (e) if it withdraws its request before the requested State has informed it of a decision to take action on the request.

Article 22

A request for proceedings, made in accordance with the provisions of this Part, shall have the effect in the requesting State of prolonging the time-limit for proceedings by six months.

SECTION 4. EFFECTS IN THE REQUESTED STATE OF A REQUEST FOR PROCEEDINGS

Article 23

If the competence of the requested State is exclusively grounded on Article 2 the time-limit for proceedings in that State shall be prolonged by six months.

Article 24

1. If proceedings are dependent on a complaint in both States the complaint brought in the requesting State shall have equal validity with that brought in the requested State.

2. If a complaint is necessary only in the requested State, that State may take proceedings even in the absence of a complaint if the person who is empowered to bring the complaint has not objected within a period of one month from the date of receipt by him of notice from the competent authority informing him of his right to object.

Article 25

In the requested State the sanction applicable to the offence shall be that prescribed by its own law unless that law provides otherwise. Where the competence of the requested State is exclusively grounded on Article 2, the sanction pronounced in that State shall not be more severe than that provided for in the law of the requesting State.

Article 26

1. Any act with a view to proceedings, taken in the requesting State in accordance with its law and regulations, shall have the same validity in the requested State as if it had been taken by the authorities of that State, provided that assimilation does not give such act a greater evidential weight than it has in the requesting State.
2. Any act which interrupts time-limitation and which has been validly performed in the requesting State shall have the same effects in the requested State and vice versa.

SECTION 5. PROVISIONAL MEASURES IN THE REQUESTED STATE

Article 27

1. When the requesting State announces its intention to transmit a request for proceedings, and if the competence of the requested State would be exclusively grounded on Article 2, the requested State may, on application by the requesting State and by virtue of this Convention, provisionally arrest the suspected person:
   (a) if the law of the requested State authorises remand in custody for the offence, and
   (b) if there are reasons to fear that the suspected person will abscond or that he will cause evidence to be suppressed.
2. The application for provisional arrest shall state that there exists a warrant of arrest or other order having the same effect, issued in accordance with the procedure laid down in the law of the requesting State; it shall also state for what offence proceedings will be requested and when and where such offence was committed and it shall contain as accurate a description of the suspected person as possible. It shall also contain a brief statement of the circumstances of the case.
3. An application for provisional arrest shall be sent direct by the authorities in the requesting State mentioned in Article 13 to the corresponding authorities in the requested State, by post or telegram or by any other means affording evidence in writing or accepted by the requested State. The requesting State shall be informed without delay of the result of its application.

Article 28

Upon receipt of a request for proceedings accompanied by the documents referred to in Article 15, paragraph 1, the requested State shall have jurisdiction to apply all such provisional measures, including remand in custody of the suspected person and seizure of property, as could be applied under its own law if the offence in respect of which proceedings are requested had been committed in its territory.

Article 29

1. The provisional measures provided in Articles 27 and 28 shall be governed by the provisions of this Convention and the law of the requested State. The law of that State, or the Convention shall also determine the conditions on which the measures may lapse.
2. These measures shall lapse in the cases referred to in Article 21, paragraph 2.
3. A person in custody shall in any event be released if he is arrested in pursuance of Article 27 and the requested State does not receive the request for proceedings within 18 days from the date of the arrest.
4. A person in custody shall in any event be released if he is arrested in pursuance of Article 27 and the documents which should accompany the request for proceedings have not been received by the requested State within 15 days from the receipt of the request for proceedings.
5. The period of custody applied exclusively by virtue of Article 27 shall not in any event exceed 40 days.

PART IV. Plurality of Criminal Proceedings

Article 30

1. Any Contracting State which, before the institution or in the course of proceedings for an offence which it considers to be neither of a political nature nor a purely military one, is aware of proceedings pending in another Contracting State against the same person in respect of the same offence shall consider whether it can either waive or suspend its own proceedings, or transfer them to the other State.
2. If it deems it advisable in the circumstances not to waive or suspend its own proceedings it shall so notify the other State in good time and in any event before judgment is given on the merits.

Article 31

1. In the eventuality referred to in Article 30, paragraph 2, the States concerned shall endeavour as far as possible to determine, after evaluation in each case of the circumstances mentioned in Article 8, which of them alone shall continue to conduct proceedings. During this consultative procedure the States concerned shall postpone judgment on the merits without however being obliged to prolong such postponement beyond a period of 30 days as from the despatch of the notification provided for in Article 30, paragraph 2.

2. The provisions of paragraph 1 shall not be binding:
   (a) on the State despatching the notification provided for in Article 30, paragraph 2, if the main trial has been declared open there in the presence of the accused before despatch of the notification;
   (b) on the State to which the notification is addressed, if the main trial has been declared open there in the presence of the accused before receipt of the notification.

Article 32
In the interests of arriving at the truth and with a view to the application of an appropriate sanction, the States concerned shall examine whether it is expedient that one of them alone shall conduct proceedings and, if so, endeavour to determine which one, when:
(a) several offences which are materially distinct and which fall under the criminal law of each of those States are ascribed either to a single person or to several persons having acted in unison;
(b) a single offence which falls under the criminal law of each of those States is ascribed to several persons having acted in unison.

Article 33
All decisions reached in accordance with Articles 31 paragraph 1, and 32 shall entail, as between the States concerned, all the consequences of a transfer of proceedings as provided for in this Convention. The State which waives its own proceedings shall be deemed to have transferred them to the other State.

Article 34
The transfer procedure provided for in Section 2 of Part III shall apply in so far as its provisions are compatible with those contained in the present Part.

PART V. Ne bis in idem

Article 35
1. A person in respect of whom a final and enforceable criminal judgment has been rendered may for the same act neither be prosecuted nor sentenced nor subjected to enforcement of a sanction in another Contracting State:
   (a) if he was acquitted;
   (b) if the sanction imposed:
      (i) has been completely enforced or is being enforced, or
      (ii) has been wholly, or with respect to the part not enforced, the subject of a pardon or an amnesty, or
      (iii) can no longer be enforced because of lapse of time;
   (c) if the court convicted the offender without imposing a sanction.
2. Nevertheless, a Contracting State shall not, unless it has itself requested the proceedings, be obliged to recognise the effect of *ne bis in idem* if the act which gave

rise to the judgment was directed against either a person or an institution or any thing having public status in that State, or if the subject of the judgment had himself a public status in that State.

3. Furthermore, a Contracting State where the act was committed or considered as such according to the law of that State shall not be obliged to recognise the effect of *ne bis in idem* unless that State has itself requested the proceedings.

Article 36
If new proceedings are instituted against a person who in another Contracting State has been sentenced for the same act, then any period of deprivation of liberty arising from the sentence enforced shall be deducted from the sanction which may be imposed.

Article 37
This Part shall not prevent the application of wider domestic provisions relating to the effect of *ne bis in idem* attached to foreign criminal judgments.

PART VI. Final Clauses

Article 38
1. This Convention shall be open to signature by the member States of the Council of Europe. It shall be subject to ratification or acceptance. Instruments of ratification or acceptance shall be deposited with the Secretary General of the Council of Europe.
2. This Convention shall enter into force three months after the date of the deposit of the third instrument of ratification or acceptance.
3. In respect of a signatory State ratifying or accepting subsequently, the Convention shall come into force three months after the date of the deposit of its instrument of ratification or acceptance.

Article 39
1. After the entry into force of this Convention, the Committee of Ministers of the Council of Europe may invite any non-member State to accede thereto provided that the resolution containing such invitation receives the unanimous agreement of the Members of the Council who have ratified the Convention.
2. Such accession shall be effected by depositing with the Secretary General of the Council of Europe an instrument of accession which shall take effect three months after the date of its deposit.

Article 40
1. Any Contracting State may, at the time of signature or when depositing its instrument of ratification, acceptance or accession, specify the territory or territories to which this Convention shall apply.

2. Any Contracting State may, when depositing its instrument of ratification, acceptance or accession or at any later date, by declaration addressed to the Secretary General of the Council of Europe, extend this Convention to any other territory or territories specified in the declaration and for whose international relations it is responsible or on whose behalf it is authorised to give undertakings.
3. Any declaration made in pursuance of the preceding paragraph may, in respect of any territory mentioned in such declaration, be withdrawn according to the procedure laid down in Article 45 of this Convention.

Article 41

1. Any Contracting State may, at the time of signature or when depositing its instrument of ratification, acceptance or accession, declare that it avails itself of one or more of the reservations provided for in Appendix I or make a declaration provided for in Appendix II to this Convention.
2. Any Contracting State may wholly or partly withdraw a reservation or declaration it has made in accordance with the foregoing paragraph by means of a declaration addressed to the Secretary General of the Council of Europe which shall become effective as from the date of its receipt.
3. A Contracting State which has made a reservation in respect of any provision of this Convention may not claim the application of that provision by any other Contracting State; it may, however, if its reservation is partial or conditional, claim the application of that provision insofar as it has itself accepted it.

Article 42

1. Any Contracting State may at any time, by declaration to the Secretary General of the Council of Europe, set out the legal provisions to be included in Appendix III to this Convention.
2. Any change of the national provisions listed in Appendix III shall be notified to the Secretary General of the Council of Europe if such a change renders the information in this Appendix incorrect.
3. Any changes made in Appendix III in application of the preceding paragraphs shall take effect in each Contracting State one month after the date of their notification by the Secretary General of the Council of Europe.

Article 43

1. This Convention affects neither the rights and the undertakings derived from extradition treaties and international multilateral conventions concerning special matters, nor provisions concerning matters which are dealt with in the present Convention and which are contained in other existing conventions between Contracting States.
2. The Contracting States may not conclude bilateral or multilateral agreements with one another on the matters dealt with in this Convention, except in order to supplement its provisions or facilitate application of the principles embodied in it.

3. Should two or more Contracting States, however, have already established their relations in this matter on the basis of uniform legislation, or instituted a special system of their own, or should they in future do so, they shall be entitled to regulate those relations accordingly, notwithstanding the terms of this Convention.
4. Contracting States ceasing to apply the terms of this Convention to their mutual relations in this matter in accordance with the provisions of the preceding paragraph shall notify the Secretary General of the Council of Europe to that effect.

Article 44

The European Committee on Crime Problems of the Council of Europe shall be kept informed regarding the application of this Convention and shall do whatever is needful to facilitate a friendly settlement of any difficulty which may arise out of its execution.

Article 45

1. This Convention shall remain in force indefinitely.
2. Any Contracting State may, insofar as it is concerned, denounce this Convention by means of a notification addressed to the Secretary General of the Council of Europe.
3. Such denunciation shall take effect six months after the date of receipt by the Secretary General of such notification.

Article 46

The Secretary General of the Council of Europe shall notify the member States of the Council and any State which has acceded to this Convention of:

(a) any signature;
(b) any deposit of an instrument of ratification, acceptance or accession;
(c) any date of entry into force of this Convention in accordance with Article 38 thereof;
(d) any declaration received in pursuance of the provisions of Article 9, paragraph 3;
(e) any declaration received in pursuance of the provisions of Article 13, paragraph 3;
(f) any declaration received in pursuance of the provisions of Article 18, paragraph 2;
(g) any declaration received in pursuance of the provisions of Article 40, paragraphs 2 and 3;
(h) any reservation or declaration made in pursuance of the provisions of Article 41, paragraph 1;
(i) the withdrawal of any reservation or declaration carried out in pursuance of the provisions of Article 41, paragraph 2;
(j) any declaration received in pursuance of Article 42, paragraph 1, and any subsequent notification received in pursuance of paragraph 2 of that Article;
(k) any notification received in pursuance of the provisions of Article 43, paragraph 4;

(I) any notification received in pursuance of the provisions of Article 45 and the date on which denunciation takes effect.

Article 47

This Convention and the notifications and declarations authorised thereunder shall apply only to offences committed after the Convention comes into effect for the Contracting States involved.

IN WITNESS WHEREOF, the undersigned, being duly authorised thereto, have signed this Convention.

DONE at Strasbourg, this 15th day of May 1972, in English and in French, both texts being equally authoritative, in a single copy, which shall remain deposited in the archives of the Council of Europe. The Secretary General shall transmit certified copies to each of the signatory and acceding Governments.

Appendix I

Each Contracting State may declare that it reserves the right:

(a) to refuse a request for proceedings, if it considers that the offence is a purely religious offence;

(b) to refuse a request for proceedings for an act the sanctions for which, in accordance with its own law, can be imposed only by an administrative authority;

(c) not to accept Article 22;

(d) not to accept Article 23;

(e) not to accept the provisions contained in the second sentence of Article 25 for constitutional reasons;

(f) not to accept the provisions laid down in Article 26, paragraph 2, where it is competent by virtue of its own law;

(g) not to apply Articles 30 and 31 in respect of an act for which the sanctions, in accordance with its own law or that of the other State concerned, can be imposed only by an administrative authority;

(h) not to accept Part V.

Annex 2 2009 Draft Framework decision on the transfer of proceedings in criminal matters

12.9.2009 EN Official Journal of the European Union C 219/7

Initiative of the Kingdom of Belgium, the Republic of Bulgaria, the Czech Republic, the Kingdom of Denmark, the Republic of Estonia, the Hellenic Republic, the Kingdom of Spain, the French Republic, the Republic of Latvia, thr Republic of Lithuania, Republic of Hungary, the Kingdom of the Netherlands, Romania, the Republic of Slovenia, the Slovak Republic and the Kingdom of Sweden for a Council Framework Decision 2009/…/JHA of … on transfer of proceedings in criminal matters

2009/C 219/03

THE COUNCIL OF THE EUROPEAN UNION,

Having regard to the Treaty on European Union, and in particular Article 31(1)(a) and Article 34(2)(b) thereof,

Having regard to the initiative of …,

Having regard to the opinion of the European Parliament (1),

Whereas:

(1) The European Union has set itself the objective of maintaining and developing an area of freedom, security and justice.

(2) The Hague Programme for strengthening freedom, security and justice in the European Union (2) requires Member States to consider possibilities of concentrating the prosecution in cross-border multilateral cases in one Member State, with a view to increasing the efficiency of prosecutions while guaranteeing the proper administration of justice.

(3) Eurojust was created to stimulate and improve the coordination of investigations and prosecutions between competent authorities of the Member States.

(4) The Council Framework Decision on prevention and settlement of conflicts of jurisdiction in criminal proceedings ([3]) addresses the adverse consequences of several Member States having criminal jurisdiction to conduct criminal proceedings (proceedings) in respect of the same facts relating to the same person. That Framework Decision establishes a procedure for exchange of information and direct consultations, aimed at preventing infringements of the *ne bis in idem* principle.

(5) Further development of judicial cooperation between Member States is needed to increase the efficiency of investigations and prosecutions. Common rules between the Member States regarding the transfer of proceedings are essential in order to address cross-border crimes. Such common rules help to prevent infringements of the *ne bis in idem* principle and support the work of Eurojust. Furthermore, in an area of freedom, security and justice there should be a common legal framework for the transfer of proceedings between Member States.

(6) Thirteen Member States have ratified and applied the European Convention on the Transfer of Proceedings in Criminal Matters of 15 May 1972. The other Member States have not ratified that convention. Some of them have relied, for the purpose of enabling other Member States to bring proceedings, on the mechanism of the European Convention on Mutual Assistance in Criminal Matters of 20 April 1959, in conjunction with the Convention on Mutual Assistance in Criminal Matters between the Member States of the European Union ([4]) of 29 May 2000. Others have used bilateral agreements or informal cooperation.

(7) An agreement between the Member States of the European Communities on the transfer of proceedings in criminal matters was signed in 1990. That agreement has, however, not entered into force due to a lack of ratifications.

(8) Consequently, no uniform procedure has been applied to cooperation between Member States regarding transfer of proceedings.

(9) This Framework Decision should establish a common legal framework for the transfer of criminal proceedings between the Member States. The measures provided for in the Framework Decision should be aimed at extending cooperation between competent authorities of the Member States with an instrument which increases efficiency in criminal proceedings and improves the proper administration of justice, by establishing common rules regulating the conditions under which criminal proceedings initiated in one Member State may be transferred to another Member State.

(10) Member States should designate the competent authorities in a way that promotes the principle of direct contacts between those authorities.

(11) For the purpose of applying this Framework Decision, a Member State could acquire competence where that competence is conferred upon the Member State by another Member State.

(12) Several Council Framework Decisions have been adopted on the application of the principle of mutual recognition to judgments in criminal matters for enforcement of sentences in other Member States, in particular Framework Decision 2005/214/JHA of 24 February 2005 on the application of the principle of mutual recognition to financial penalties (5), Framework Decision 2008/909/JHA of 27 November 2008 on the application of the principle of mutual recognition to judgments in criminal matters imposing custodial sentences or measures involving deprivation of liberty for the purpose of their enforcement in the European Union (6) and Framework Decision 2008/947/JHA of 27 November 2008 on the application of the principle of mutual recognition to judgments and probation decisions with a view to the supervision of probation measures and alternative sanctions (7). This Framework Decision should supplement the provisions of those Framework Decisions and should not be interpreted as precluding their application.

(13) The legitimate interests of suspects and victims should be taken into account in applying this Framework Decision. Nothing in this Framework Decision should, however, be interpreted as undermining the prerogative of the competent judicial authorities to determine whether proceedings will be transferred.

(14) Nothing in this Framework Decision should be interpreted as affecting any right of individuals to argue that they should be prosecuted in their own or in another jurisdiction if such a right exists under national law.

(15) The competent authorities should be encouraged to consult each other before a transfer of proceedings is requested and whenever it is felt appropriate to facilitate the smooth and efficient application of this Framework Decision.

(16) When proceedings have been transferred in accordance with this Framework Decision, the receiving authority should apply its national law and procedures.

(17) This Framework Decision does not constitute a legal basis for arresting persons with a view to their physical transfer to another Member State so that the latter can bring proceedings against the person.

(18) This Framework Decision respects the fundamental rights and observes the principles recognised by Article 6 of the Treaty on European Union and reflected

by the Charter of Fundamental Rights of the European Union, in particular Chapter VI thereof. Nothing in this Framework Decision should be interpreted as prohibiting a refusal to cooperate when there are objective reasons to believe that proceedings have been initiated for the purpose of punishing a person on the grounds of his or her sex, race, religion, ethnic origin, nationality, language, political opinions or sexual orientation, or that that person's position may be prejudiced on any one of those grounds,

HAS ADOPTED THIS FRAMEWORK DECISION:

CHAPTER 1
GENERAL PROVISIONS

Article 1
Objective and scope
The purpose of this Framework Decision is to increase efficiency in criminal proceedings and to improve the proper administration of justice within the area of freedom, security and justice by establishing common rules facilitating the transfer of criminal proceedings between competent authorities of the Member States, taking into account the legitimate interests of suspects and victims.

Article 2
Fundamental rights
This Framework Decision shall not have the effect of modifying the obligations to respect the fundamental rights and principles recognised by Article 6 of the Treaty on European Union.

Article 3
Definitions
For the purposes of this Framework Decision:

(a) 'offence' shall mean an act constituting an offence pursuant to national criminal law;

(b) 'transferring authority' shall mean an authority which is competent to request transfer of proceedings;

(c) 'receiving authority' shall mean an authority which is competent to receive a request for transfer of proceedings.

Article 4
Designation of competent authorities

1. Each Member State shall inform the General Secretariat of the Council which judicial authorities, under its national law, are competent to act as transferring authority and receiving authority (competent authorities) pursuant to this Framework Decision.
2. Member States may designate non-judicial authorities as the competent authorities for taking decisions under this Framework Decision, provided that such authorities have competence for taking decisions of a similar nature under their national law and procedures.
3. Each Member State may, if necessary due to the organisation of its internal system, designate one or more central authorities to assist the competent authorities with the administrative transmission and reception of the requests. It shall inform the General Secretariat of the Council thereof.
4. The General Secretariat of the Council shall make the information received available to all Member States and the Commission.

Article 5
Competence

1. For the purpose of applying this Framework Decision, any Member State shall have competence to prosecute, under its national law, any offence to which the law of another Member State is applicable.
2. The competence conferred on a Member State exclusively by virtue of paragraph 1 may be exercised only pursuant to a request for transfer of proceedings.

Article 6
Waiver of proceedings

Any Member State having competence under its national law to prosecute an offence may, for the purposes of applying this Framework Decision, waive or desist from proceedings against a suspected person, in order to allow for the transfer of proceedings in respect of that offence to another Member State.

CHAPTER 2
TRANSFER OF PROCEEDINGS

Article 7
Criteria for requesting transfer of proceedings

When a person is suspected of having committed an offence under the law of a Member State, the transferring authority of that Member State may request the receiving authority in another Member State to take the proceedings if that would improve the efficient and proper administration of justice, and if at least one of the following criteria is met:

(a) the offence has been committed wholly or partly in the territory of the other Member State, or most of the effects or a substantial part of the damage caused by the offence was sustained in the territory of the other Member State;

(b) the suspected person is ordinarily resident in the other Member State;

(c) substantial parts of the most important evidence are located in the other Member State;

(d) there are ongoing proceedings against the suspected person in the other Member State;

(e) there are ongoing proceedings in respect of the same or related facts involving other persons, in particular in respect of the same criminal organisation, in the other Member State;

(f) the suspected person is serving or is to serve a sentence involving deprivation of liberty in the other Member State;

(g) enforcement of the sentence in the other Member State is likely to improve the prospects for social rehabilitation of the person sentenced or there are other reasons for a more appropriate enforcement of the sentence in the other Member State; or

(h) the victim is ordinarily resident in the other Member State or the victim has another significant interest in having the proceedings transferred.

Article 8
Informing the suspected person
Before a request for transfer is made, the transferring authority shall, where appropriate and in accordance with national law, inform the person suspected of the offence of the intended transfer. If the suspected person presents an opinion on the transfer, the transferring authority shall inform the receiving authority thereof.

Article 9
The rights of the victim
Before a request for transfer is made the transferring authority shall give due consideration to the interests of the victim of the offence and see to it that their rights under national law are fully respected. This includes, in particular, a right for the victim to be informed of the intended transfer.

Article 10
Procedure for requesting transfer of proceedings

1. Before the transferring authority makes a request for transfer of proceedings in accordance with Article 7, it may inform and consult with the receiving authority, in particular as regards whether the receiving authority is likely to invoke one of the grounds for refusal referred to in Article 12.
2. To consult with the receiving authority in accordance with paragraph 1, the transferring authority shall make information regarding the proceedings available to the receiving authority and may provide it in writing, using a standard form set out in the Annex.
3. The form referred to in paragraph 2 shall be forwarded by the transferring authority directly to the receiving authority by any means that leave a written record under conditions that allow the receiving authority to establish its authenticity. All other official communications shall also be made directly between those authorities.
4. A request for transfer shall be accompanied by the original or by a certified copy of the criminal file or relevant parts thereof, by any other relevant documents and by a copy of the relevant legislation, or, where this is not possible, by a statement of the relevant law. If consultation has not taken place in accordance with the procedure referred to in paragraph 3, the request for transfer shall be made in writing, using the standard form set out in the Annex, in accordance with the procedure referred to in paragraph 3.
5. The transferring authority shall inform the receiving authority of any procedural acts or measures with a bearing on the proceedings that have been undertaken in the Member State of the transferring authority after the transmission of the request. This communication shall be accompanied by all relevant documents.
6. The transferring authority may withdraw the request for transfer at any time prior to the receiving authority's decision under Article 13(1) to accept transfer.
7. If the receiving authority is not known to the transferring authority, the latter shall make all necessary inquiries, including through the contact points of the European Judicial Network, in order to obtain the details of the receiving authority.
8. If the authority which receives the request is not the competent authority under Article 4, it shall transmit the request *ex officio* to the competent authority and shall without delay inform the transferring authority accordingly.

Article 11
Double criminality

A request for transfer of proceedings can be complied with only if the act underlying the request for transfer constitutes an offence under the law of the Member State of the receiving authority.

Article 12
Grounds for refusal

1. The receiving authority of a Member State may refuse transfer only:
   (a) if the act does not constitute an offence under the law of that Member State in accordance with Article 11;
   (b) if taking proceedings would be contrary to the *ne bis in idem* principle;
   (c) if the suspect cannot be held criminally liable for the offence due to his or her age;
   (d) if there is an immunity or privilege under the law of that Member State which makes it impossible to take action;
   (e) where the criminal prosecution is statute-barred in accordance with the law of that Member State;
   (f) if the offence is covered by amnesty in accordance with the law of that Member State;
   (g) if the criteria on which the request is based under Article 7 points (a) to (h) are not considered met.
2. If the competence of the Member State which received the request is exclusively grounded on Article 5, the receiving authority may, in addition to the grounds for refusal in paragraph 1, refuse transfer if it is not considered to improve the efficient and proper administration of justice.
3. In the cases referred to in paragraph 1(g), before deciding to refuse transfer, the receiving authority shall communicate, by appropriate means, with the transferring authority and, where necessary, ask it to supply without delay all additional information required.

Article 13
Decision of the receiving authority

1. When a request for transfer of proceedings has been received, the receiving authority shall without undue delay determine whether a transfer of proceedings will be accepted and shall, unless it decides to invoke one of the grounds for refusal in Article 12, take all necessary measures to comply with the request under its national law.
2. The receiving authority shall without delay inform the transferring authority, by any means that leave a written record, of its decision. If the receiving authority decides to refuse transfer, it shall inform the transferring authority of the reasons for its decision.

Article 14
Consultations between the transferring and receiving authorities

The transferring and receiving authorities may, where and whenever it is felt appropriate, consult each other with a view to facilitating the smooth and efficient application of this Framework Decision.

Article 15

Cooperation with Eurojust and the European Judicial Network

Any competent authority may, at any stage of the procedure, request the assistance of Eurojust or the European Judicial Network.

CHAPTER 3
EFFECTS OF THE TRANSFER

Article 16

Effects in the Member State of the transferring authority

1. At the latest upon receipt of the notification of the acceptance by the receiving authority of a transfer of proceedings, the proceedings related to the facts underlying the request for transfer shall, in accordance with national law, be suspended or discontinued in the Member State of the transferring authority, except for any necessary investigations, including judicial assistance to the receiving authority.
2. The transferring authority may open or reopen proceedings if the receiving authority informs it of its decision to discontinue the proceedings related to the facts underlying the request.
3. The transferring authority may not open or reopen proceedings if it has been informed by the receiving authority of a decision delivered at the end of the proceedings in the Member State of the receiving authority, if that decision presents an obstacle to further proceedings under the law of that Member State.
4. This Framework Decision is without prejudice to the right of victims to initiate criminal proceedings against the offender, when so provided for by national law.

Article 17

Effects in the Member State of the receiving authority

1. The proceedings transferred shall be governed by the law of the Member State to which transfer has been effected.
2. Where compatible with the law of the Member State of the receiving authority, any act for the purpose of proceedings or preparatory inquiries performed in the Member State of the transferring authority or any act interrupting or suspending the period of limitation shall have the same validity in the other Member State as if it had been validly performed in or by the authorities of that Member State.
3. When the receiving authority has decided to accept a transfer of proceedings, it may apply any procedural measures permitted under its national law.
4. If proceedings are dependent on a complaint in both Member States, the complaint brought in the Member State of the transferring authority shall have equal validity with that brought in the other Member State.
5. Where only the law of the Member State of the receiving authority requires that a complaint be lodged or another means of initiating proceedings be employed, those formalities shall be carried out within the time limits laid down by the law of that Member State. The other Member State shall be informed thereof. The

time limit shall start to run on the date on which the receiving authority decides to accept a transfer of proceedings.

6. In the Member State of the receiving authority the sanction applicable to the offence shall be that prescribed by its own law unless that law provides otherwise. Where the competence is exclusively grounded on Article 5, the sanction pronounced in that Member State shall not be more severe than that provided for in the law of the other Member State.

CHAPTER 4
FINAL PROVISIONS

Article 18
Information to be given by the receiving authority

The receiving authority shall inform the transferring authority of the discontinuation of proceedings or of any decision delivered at the end of the proceedings, including whether that decision presents an obstacle to further proceedings under the law of the Member State of the receiving authority, or of other information of substantial value. It shall forward a copy of the written decision.

Article 19
Languages

1. The form set out in the Annex and the relevant parts of the criminal file shall be translated into the official language or one of the official languages of the Member State to which they are forwarded.
2. Any Member State may, upon the adoption of this Framework Decision or later, state in a declaration deposited with the General Secretariat of the Council that it will accept a translation into one or more other official languages of the institutions of the European Union. The General Secretariat shall make that information available to the other Member States and the Commission.

Article 20
Costs

Costs resulting from the application of this Framework Decision shall be borne by the Member State of the receiving authority, except for costs arising exclusively in the territory of the other Member State.

Article 21
Relationship with other agreements and arrangements

1. In relations between Member States that are bound by the European Convention on the Transfer of Proceedings in Criminal Matters of 15 May 1972, the provisions of this Framework Decision shall apply instead of the corresponding provisions of that Convention from the date referred to in Article 22(1).

2. Member States may continue to apply bilateral or multilateral agreements or arrangements in force, insofar as they allow the objectives of this Framework Decision to be extended or help to further simplify or facilitate the transfer of proceedings.
3. Member States may conclude bilateral or multilateral agreements or arrangements after the entry into force of this Framework Decision insofar as such agreements or arrangements allow the provisions of this Framework Decision to be extended and help to simplify or facilitate further the transfer of proceedings.
4. Member States shall notify the Council and the Commission by [...] of the agreements and arrangements referred to in paragraph 2 which they wish to continue applying. Member States shall also notify the Council and the Commission of any agreement or arrangement referred to in paragraph 3, within three months of signing it.

Article 22
Implementation

1. Member States shall take the necessary measures to comply with the provisions of this Framework Decision by [...].
2. Member States shall transmit to the General Secretariat of the Council and the Commission the text of the provisions transposing into their national law the obligations imposed on them under this Framework Decision.

Article 23
Entry into force

This Framework Decision shall enter into force on the day of its publication in the *Official Journal of the European Union*.
Done at, ...

For the Council
The President
...

(1) Opinion of ...
(2) OJ C 53, 3.3.2005, p. 1.
(3) 8535/09.
(4) OJ C 197, 12.7.2000, p. 3.
(5) OJ L 76, 22.3.2005, p. 16.
(6) OJ L 327, 5.12.2008, p. 27.
(7) OJ L 337, 16.12.2008, p. 102.

ANNEX

FORM FOR TRANSFER OF CRIMINAL PROCEEDINGS

(referred to in Article 10 of Framework Decision 2009/…/JHA)

This form is used as:

☐ a means to inform and consult regarding a possible transfer of proceedings

☐ a request for transfer of proceedings

Member State of the transferring authority:

Member State of the receiving authority:

Transferring authority (or other authority referred to in Article 4) — contact details:

Name: ……………………………………………………………………………………

Address: ……………………………………………………………………………………

Tel. (country code) (area/city code): ……………………………………………………………………………………

Fax (country code) (area/city code): ……………………………………………………………………………………

Details of the person(s) to be contacted:

Name: ……………………………………………………………………………………

Position (title/grade): ……………………………………………………………………………………

File reference: ……………………………………………………………………………………

Tel. (country code) (area/city code): ……………………………………………………………………………………

Fax (country code) (area/city code): ……………………………………………………………………………………

E-mail (if any): ……………………………………………………………………………………

The receiving authority which has been consulted:

Name: ....

Address: ....

☐ No consultation has been made.

Details of the person(s) contacted, if the receiving authority has been consulted:

Name: ....

Position (title/grade): ....

File reference (if known): ....

Tel. (country code) (area/city code): ....

Fax (country code) (area/city code): ....

E-mail (if any): ....

Details of the suspected person(s):

Name: ....

Nationality: ....

Date of birth: ....

Place of birth: ....

Identity number or social security number (if any):

Address: ....

Language(s) understood (if known): ....

☐ The suspected person has been informed about the intended transfer.

☐ The suspected person has presented an opinion on the intended transfer. The opinion of the suspected person:

Description of facts of the alleged offence(s) (including where, when and how it was committed):

Nature and legal classification of the alleged offence(s):

☐ The criminal file or its certified copy is enclosed.

☐ Relevant parts of the criminal file or their certified copies are enclosed.

☐ A copy of the relevant legislation is enclosed.

☐ A copy of the relevant legislation is not enclosed. A statement of applicable legislation:

Criteria for requesting transfer of proceedings:

☐ the offence has been committed wholly or partly in the territory of the Member State of the receiving authority;

☐ most of the effects or substantial part of the damage caused by the offence was sustained in the territory of the Member State of the receiving authority;

☐ the suspected person is ordinarily resident in the Member State of the receiving authority;

☐ substantial parts of the most important evidence are located in the Member State of the receiving authority;

☐ there are ongoing proceedings against the suspected person in the Member State of the receiving authority;

☐ there are ongoing proceedings in respect of the same or related facts involving other persons, in particular in respect of the same criminal organisation, in the Member State of the receiving authority;

☐ the suspected person is serving or is to serve a sentence involving deprivation of liberty in the Member State of the receiving authority;

☐ enforcement of the sentence in the Member State of the receiving authority is likely to improve the prospects for social rehabilitation of the person sentenced;

☐ there are other reasons for a more appropriate enforcement of the sentence in the Member State of the receiving authority.

Please indicate the reasons:

☐ the victim is ordinarily resident in the Member State of the receiving authority;

☐ the victim has another significant interest in having the proceedings transferred.

Please indicate the reason:

Stage of the proceedings that has been reached, including any procedural acts taken in the Member State of the transferring authority:

Information about evidence collected so far:

Details of the victim(s) (if applicable):

Name: ....

Nationality: ....

Date of birth: ....

Place of birth: ....

Identity number or social security number (if any):

Address: ....

Language(s) understood (if known): ....

Other details of interest: ....

☐ The victim has been informed about the intended transfer.

Additional information:
☐ Other relevant documents have been enclosed, namely:

Signature, date and official stamp: